QUICK-TO-FIX
DESSERTS

QUICK-TO-FIX
DESSERTS

for Foodservice Menu Planning

Eulalia C. Blair

CBI

CBI Publishing Company, Inc.
51 Sleeper Street, Boston, Massachusetts 02210

Compositor: Jay's Publishers Services, Inc.
Cover Designer: Charles G. Mitchell

Cover Photos: Love Cake Saronno (*main image*) courtesy of Amaretto di Saronno; H'a Penny Pudding Cake (*upper inset*) courtesy of Cling Peach Advisory Board; Strawberry Daiquiri Pie (*central inset*) courtesy of California Strawberry Advisory Board; Spiced Hot Fruit Compote (*lower inset*) courtesy of *Institutions/Volume Feeding Management* Magazine.

Library of Congress Cataloging in Publication Data

Blair, Eulalia C
   Quick-to-fix desserts for foodservice menu planning.

   Includes index.
   1. Desserts. 2. Quantity cookery. I. Title.
TX773.B55   641.8'6   80-13124
ISBN 0-8436-2183-4

Printed in the United States

Printing (*last digit*): 9 8 7 6 5 4 3 2 1

Contents

Acknowledgments

I SHOULD LIKE to express my sincere appreciation to the many people who have had a part in the making of this book.

I am greatly indebted to the resourceful home economists and food technicians who, working in various test kitchens, developed many of the recipes selected for these pages. They richly deserve my special thanks.

I am also extremely grateful to my friends and colleagues with food processors, manufacturers, public relations firms, advertising agencies, associations, and institutions. They have been most generous in giving their counsel, sharing their ideas, and, most important, in making recipe material available for use in Volume Feeding Management, *both during the years of its separate publication and later after it was combined with* Institutions Magazine. *These recipes form the nucleus of this collection. Now, once again, these friends have cheerfully obliged by supplying photographs to illustrate this book.*

In addition, my thanks go to the many foodservice operators who have participated in the making of this book by providing favorite recipes from their files.

I want to say another meaningful "Thank You" to Jule Wilkinson for taking on the task of editing this book. I deeply appreciate having the benefit of her guidance as well as her expert hand at editing and carrying out many of the details that publishing involves. As always, it has been a pleasure to work with her in producing this book.

Eulalia C. Blair

Introduction

THIS NEW and a-little-bit-different book of desserts is planned to help foodservice operators cope with today's pressure for time. It clearly is intended for the enterprising crowd who want an easy, speedy means to extend the menu and offer exciting desserts—specialties that will dazzle and sell.

To help in achieving this end, this book offers some two hundred and fifty recipes—plus numerous imaginative serving ideas—all carefully selected for ease of preparation and demonstrated appeal. Among the collection are quick-to-fix desserts based on fruit and others, just as easy, that employ ice cream. Many recipes take advantage of purchased baked goods (pie shells, cake layers, angel food cakes, and similar items) or their equivalents made on-premise in advance. Other recipes can be partly prepared ahead of scheduled service, then left to complete their preparation in refrigerator or freezer, to be readily accessible at serving time. Included are recipes for chiffon, ice cream, and other open-face pies; a wide assortment of unusual puddings and gelatine treats; no-bake cheesecakes; and easy-to-assemble delicacies fashioned with cake.

To supplement all this is a section devoted to toppings, fillings, sauces, and glazes. Throughout this book you'll find an impressive galaxy of ideas, arranged in lists, on garnishes, make-up tricks, and new ways to give popular favorites distinction and romance. Included are ways to:

- Increase the drama of cheesecake with garnishes.
- Vary the service of clear, sparkling gelatines.
- Give variety to simple puddings.
- Add extra excitement to ubiquitous ice cream offerings.
- Create glamorous desserts using plain angel food or layers of cake.
- Employ various enhancements to give importance to fruit.

- Add originality and sparkle to pies that come ready-to-bake or to thaw-and-serve.
- Team the long line of dessert cheeses with companionable crackers and fruit.

Sunkist Growers

Carefree Inn Orange Meringue Surprise

Orange shells filled with liqueur-flavored ice cream are then topped with meringue and baked a la Alaska. Bake ahead, freeze, and hold; thaw about 15 minutes before serving.

FRUIT DESSERTS

Fresh Fruit

FRESH FRUIT, fancifully presented, stands out as one of the world's simplest dishes, yet one of the best. Fruits that are well-ripened and ready for eating promise zest and refreshment; they speak for themselves.

Fruit Elegance, Easy to Arrange

Fresh fruit requires neither cooking nor special tricks. A bit of smart showmanship, though, multiplies the charm. Unusual serving equipment, garnishes, and unexpected arrangements can do a lot. Even the style in which fruit is cut can make a big difference.

INNOVATIVE SERVING IDEAS

Alternating layers of two cut-up fruits, such as halved strawberries and pineapple cubes or sliced peaches and red raspberries, in a tall parfait glass

Ambrosia, plain or fancy (see pages 9 and 23–25)

An assortment of whole fruits on a tray presented with cheese

Bananas with cream that contains a suspicion of nutmeg

Cantaloupe circles with cubes of lime gelatin

Dark sweet cherries on stems

Halved fresh figs with Creme Fraiche (recipe page 287)

Grapefruit halves, chilled or broiled (see pages 7–8)

Grapefruit sections with a scattering of pomegranate seeds

Two half-portions of fruit, such as grapefruit sections with halved strawberries or sliced peaches with blueberries, unmixed, dished-up side-by-side in a flat nappy-type dish

Melon balls, fresh pineapple cubes, banana chunks, and whole strawberries threaded on skewers

Melon balls in sauterne

Orange sections splashed with Curacao

Fresh pineapple cubes with rum

Pineapple fans with snipped fresh mint

Sliced strawberries in orange juice

Unhulled strawberries in a small basket lined with leaves with a dish of powdered sugar for dipping

Triangles of peeled watermelon with feta cheese

CHILLED GRAPEFRUIT HALVES

Vary the garnishes:

Galax leaves

A sprig or bits of chopped mint

A cube of mint jelly or a cube each of currant and mint

Crushed after-dinner mints

Red or green maraschino cherry (whole; slices; slivers; chopped; whole, on stem)

A scattering of pomegranate seeds

A small bunch of plain or frosted grapes (try "frosting" with cinnamon sugar)

Halves of seeded grapes

Assorted small melon balls, with or without mint

Crushed pineapple

Diced frozen peaches

A spoonful of just-thawed frozen, sliced strawberries

A whole fresh strawberry with its bright green cap

Orange sections, whole or diced

A twisted, unpeeled orange slice

Thinly sliced preserved kumquats

A small scoop of pineapple, lemon, orange, lime, raspberry, or cranberry sherbet

BROILED OR CHILLED GRAPEFRUIT HALVES

Flavor with wines and liqueurs:

  Sherry
  Claret
  Port
  Madeira
  Sweet Italian vermouth
  Rum
  Kirsch
  Curacao
  Creme de Menthe

Frosted Service for Grapefruit Sections

BROILED GRAPEFRUIT HALVES

Vary the spice:
Nutmeg
Cinnamon
Mace
Ground cloves
Cardamon

Vary the sweetening:
White, brown, or cinnamon sugar
Honey
Maple sugar or syrup
Orange marmalade
Light molasses
Mashed mint, currant, apple or quince jelly

AMBROSIA

THE BASIC AMBROSIA combination is orange sections layered with coconut and a sprinkling of sugar. Use light brown sugar for a slightly varied taste.

Additions for an Exotic Touch:
Grand Marnier
Curacao
Triple Sec

Other Likely Additions:
Grapefruit sections
Grapefruit and tangerine sections
Sliced banana
Pineapple chunks
Pitted bing cherries
Cut-up dates
Diced apple, banana, and dates
Strawberries or blueberries
Canned fruit cocktail
A topping of orange, lemon, or pineapple sherbet

Fruit And Ice Cream Or Sherbet

APPEALING COMBINATIONS

Warm, spiced applesauce a la mode

Baked apple halves a la mode

Baked apple half prepared as an individual apple Alaska

Cantaloupe half with lime sherbet or vanilla ice cream

Fruit cup topped with sherbet

A parfait of halved seedless grapes, lemon sherbet, and diced, roasted almonds

Cling Peach Advisory Board

Ice Cream, Sherbet—Extra Appeal for Fruit

Peach halves, vanilla ice cream, and raspberry or Melba sauce

Sliced, sweetened, fresh peaches topped with pistachio, strawberry, or butter pecan ice cream

Sliced peaches and seedless grapes with raspberry sherbet

Peach halves, vanilla ice cream, and a topping of thinned apricot jam and shaved Brazil nuts or sliced almonds

Broiled, canned peach halves a la mode

Pear halves, vanilla ice cream, and hot chocolate sauce

Pear halves, cranberry sherbet

Chilled pear halves, butter pecan ice cream, and butterscotch sauce

Pear halves, lemon sherbet, and a generous splash of Creme de Menthe

Pears, peppermint stick ice cream, and drizzles of chocolate sauce

Pineapple tidbits topped with a coconut-wrapped ball of ice cream

MANY WARM, HOME-LIKE fruit desserts can be fashioned with peaches, such as the following peach pleasers.

Peach halves or slices are delicious when gently heated in their own syrup, then presented with unwhipped cream, a spoonful of sour cream, or whipped cream with chopped roasted almonds folded in.

Peaches and their syrup can also be heated with one of the following additions: wine, spices, grated orange or lemon peel, or finely chopped, candied ginger.

Peach slices gain a special touch when heated with thin slices of orange, sugar, and rum, then served over babas.

Cling Peach Advisory Board

Peaches Flambe—Fruit-Starred Dessert

Filled Fruit

A BRAND NEW DIMENSION comes to fruit with the imaginative use of fillings. They create distinctive desserts; feature them with pride. Suggestions to try:

Fresh pears, quartered and cored, dipped in lemon juice, and filled with a mixture of blue and cream cheese

Cantaloupe halves filled with red raspberries or blueberries

Honeydew wedges heaped with a mixture of fruit, such as sliced peaches, blueberries, and stemmed seedless grapes

Fresh pineapple (hollowed-out halves or quarters, cut through the bright green top) filled with a medley of cut, fresh fruit tossed with coconut and bits of preserved ginger

Apples baked with a filling of mincemeat or a mixture of raisins, walnuts, and dates

Whole cinnamon apples filled with softened cream cheese (See recipe for Rosy Cinnamon Apples page 41)

Western Growers Association

Melange of Melon

13

Orange shells filled with orange sherbet or vanilla ice cream with Triple Sec or other orange-flavored liqueur added and a garnish of whole fresh strawberries and a green leaf or two (To prepare: Cut top from oranges; remove fruit. Cut a saw-toothed edge around shells; freeze. Fill the frozen shells with sherbet or ice cream; hold in freezer. Add strawberry garnish when ready to serve.)

Baked cling peach halves have special variety. Try them with fillings of:

Coconut and honey
Brown sugar, cinnamon, and butter
Mincemeat
Chopped, roasted almonds, and currant jelly
Chopped dates and orange juice
Macaroon crumbs moistened with sherry
Raisins and orange marmalade
Prunes, dates, and chopped nuts or raspberry jam

SAUCE MAGIC adds savor to fruits—fresh, frozen, canned, or dried—giving them menu status as full-fledged, high-style desserts. Some sauced fruits are at their best warm, others chilled. Some sauces complement a number of fruits, others are more selective. But all offer promise of delicious desserts. With today's choice of fruits and easy-to-make sauces, operators can always have a selection of desserts on hand that are practically ready-to-go.

Cling Peach Advisory Board

Raspberry-Sauced Fruit in Carnival Colors

Fruit With Sauce

FRUIT—SAUCE COMBINATIONS

Apples:

Warm, fresh applesauce with sherried hard sauce

Baked apples with hot mincemeat sauce

Apple quarters cooked with dates, topped with bourbon nutmeg sauce

Baked apple with eggnog sauce

Baked apples or canned pears sauced with softened butter pecan ice cream that has been blended with cognac

Apricots:

Apricot halves with eggnog or sabayon sauce

Canned, whole apricots with softened ice cream that has been laced with apricot brandy

Cooked, dried apricots and prunes with almond-flavored custard sauce

Bananas:

Bananas in custard sauce, garnished with shaved chocolate or toasted, slivered almonds

Sliced bananas with nutmeg-scented pineapple sauce

Baked bananas with a rich orange sauce

Bananas with whipped cream, chocolate sauce

Bananas with fresh strawberry and rhubarb sauce

Hot baked bananas with flaming rum sauce

Sliced bananas sauced with a blend of orange juice and pureed strawberries

Blueberries:

Blueberries with maple syrup, a dollop of sour cream

Cherries:

Ice-cold, frozen red cherries with sour cream (See recipe page 37.)

Grapefruit:

Grapefruit sections or banana chunks sauced with not-quite-
thawed frozen, sliced strawberries

Grapes:

Seedless white grapes, whole or halved, with sour cream
and a sprinkling of brown sugar or bits of candied ginger

Melon:

Assorted melon balls with a fresh mint sauce

Cantaloupe and honeydrew balls in a light simple syrup
spiked with lime

Nectarines:

Fresh nectarines or peaches with sabayon sauce (See recipe
page 33.)

Oranges:

Orange sections with chilled custard sauce

Orange sections with brandied bing cherry sauce

Peaches:

Canned peach halves sauced with softened cream cheese,
garnished with a dab of raspberry jelly or preserves

Peach halves in almond custard sauce, a scattering of
toasted slivered almonds across the top (See recipe for
Dessert Aphrodite page 34.)

Baked, canned, peach halves (topped with meringue and
sprinkled with chopped almonds) served with sherried
custard sauce

Oven-warmed canned peach slices with spiced hard sauce

Pears:

Pear halves with honey-lime sauce (honey thinned with
fresh lime juice and flecked with bits of lime and preserved ginger)

Coddled whole fresh pears in spiced rum sauce (See recipe
page 32.)

Pears with butterscotch sauce and toasted pecans

Pear halves with raspberry sherbet, sauced with sweetened, sliced strawberries

Baked, canned, pear halves (topped with meringue and sprinkled with chopped walnuts), hot lemon sauce

Pineapple:

Fresh pineapple slices with sweetened, sliced strawberry sauce

Pineapple fritters (drained, canned, pineapple slices dipped in fritter batter and deep fried) served with sabayon, Melba, or a thin lemon sauce

Chilled, drained, canned, pineapple chunks with orange—sour cream sauce

Plums:

Green gage plums with sherried custard sauce

Chilled, canned, purple plums sauced with sour cream

Prunes:

Prunes combined with mandarin orange sections and served warm with orange foamy sauce

Prunes with cold, whipped, custard sauce

Prunes topped with vanilla ice cream (softened to sauce consistency)

Prune and apricot compote with sabayon sauce

Raspberries:

Red raspberries with softened vanilla ice cream blended with Framboise

Strawberries:

Halved, sweetened strawberries and pineapple chunks marinated in Kirsch, sauced with raspberry puree

Strawberries with Romanoff sauce

Strawberries with softened vanilla ice cream blended with a light touch of Kirsch

Many sauce recipes can be found among the fruit recipes in this book (pages 3-54):

Cold Whipped Custard Sauce
Spiced Rum Sauce
Almond Custard Sauce
Sabayon Sauce

and others can be found in the "Crowning Touches" section (pages 263-294):

Creme Fraiche
Orange-Sour Cream Sauce
Eggnog Sauce
Mincemeat Sauce
Fresh Strawberry and Rhubarb Sauce
Lemon Sauce

Another fruitful source of sauce recipes is Garnishes, Relishes, and Sauces for Foodservice Menu Planning[1] :

Rich Orange Sauce
Orange Foamy Sauce
Pacific Rum Sauce
Romanoff Sauce
Bourbon Nutmeg Sauce
Sabayon Sauce
Honey Lime Ginger Sauce
Melba Sauce
Nutmeg Pineapple Sauce
Butterscotch Sauce
Custard Sauces
Lemon Sauce

---

1. Eulalia C. Blair, *Garnishes, Relishes, and Sauces for Foodservice Menu Planning,* CBI Publishing Co. Inc. (Boston, *1977*).

Spirited Fruit Desserts

WINES AND LIQUEURS add a master touch to fresh, canned, or frozen fruits and can be used to great advantage in producing simple but extraordinary desserts. Kirsch, a liqueur distilled from cherries, has a bitter almond flavor of its own which is complementary to all fruits. Sherry, rum, and brandy as well, also enhance the flavor of apricots, cherries, peaches, pears, pineapple, and plums.

When the dessert is to be presented cold, allow the fruit and wine or liqueur combination to stand for an hour or more before serving to blend and mellow the flavors.

- Let canned pear halves refrigerate for several hours in equal parts of their syrup and port wine. Or use equal parts of pear syrup and Creme de Cacao for the marinade and top the combination with whipped cream and a dusting of powdered instant coffee.
- Combine drained, pitted dark sweet cherries with peeled oranges (cut in bite-size pieces and lightly sugared). Add rum and fresh lime juice, then complete the sweetening with grenadine.
- Let canned figs mingle for an hour or so with sherry or brandy and a dash of lemon juice to round out the taste.
- Marinate bite-size pieces of peeled oranges in Curacao for several hours. Present fruit and some of the marinade in sherbet-lined champagne glasses. If desired, top with a sugar cube saturated with lemon or orange extract and set it aflame (see picture, p. 79.)

To prepare the shells, line chilled champagne or stemmed dessert dishes with slightly softened lemon or orange sherbet. Using the back of a tablespoon, mold sherbet on bottom and up sides of glasses to a depth of 1/4 inch. (The edge may be smoothed with a table knife after sherbet is refrozen.) Put each shell in freezer immediately after molding.

Well-flavored fruit desserts served warm—or warm and aflame, for drama—add an element of pleasant expectancy for the diner.

- Fill peach or pear halves with nuts, candied fruits, macaroon crumbs, or coconut. Bake, basting with sherry or rum.
- Bake peaches with brandy and honey. Serve with nutmeg-scented whipped cream.
- Cook canned peaches or apricots to reduce the syrup. Blaze peaches with brandy or bourbon; apricots with brandy or Kirsch.
- Bake peaches with maple syrup laced with brandy or brandy and Kirsch. Serve with a foamy dessert sauce.

Fruit Compotes

FRUITS SERVED as compotes strike a note of glamor and make an elegant finale to a meal. Yet well-put-together combinations are simply a matter of minutes and a little creative thought. Here are a Dozen Suggestions to Lead the Way:

- Combine drained purple plums with undrained greengage plums; add sherry; chill.
- Arrange groupings of apricot halves, royal anne cherries, and grapefruit sections in a flat, open dessert dish.
- Heat syrup from canned figs with grated lemon peel, cinnamon, and nutmeg. Pour over drained figs, canned apricots, and cooked dried prunes. Chill. Add a light touch of rum at serving time.

*California Apricot Advisory Board/
National Cherry Growers and Industries Foundation*

Medley of Flavors in Mixed Fruit Compote

- Arrange canned sliced peaches, pineapple chunks, and fresh blueberries side by side in a serving dish. Top with sherry-flavored sour cream and a sprinkling of brown sugar.
- Mix pineapple juice with frozen concentrated lemonade; pour over drained purple plums and pears. Chill.
- Arrange a small whole pear, whole canned apricot, and a greengage plum in a serving dish. Spoon in a few dark cherries.
- Serve prunes, hothouse rhubarb, and sliced bananas together, arranging them in a flat, nappy-type dish.
- Garnish an arrangement of sliced peaches, pear half, and pineapple chunks with a twisted slice of lime.
- Combine chilled peaches, apricots, and pears. Serve topped with whipped cream in which brown sugar, mint jelly, or crushed red raspberries have been folded.
- Arrange purple plums and canned figs with thick half slices of orange (rind on). Garnish with toasted slivered almonds.
- Arrange half slices of pineapple with a large, plump stewed prune and canned apricot halves.
- Arrange groupings of mandarin orange sections, dark cherries, and pineapple tidbits in a nappy-type dish.

AMBROSIA

Yield: 23 portions

Ingredients

ORANGES, 126 size	18
COCONUT, FRESH, grated	9-1/2 ounces
BANANAS, diced	1-1/2 pounds
MARASCHINO CHERRY RINGS	23

Procedure

1. Chill, wash, peel, and section oranges.
2. Peel and grate fresh coconut to make required amount.
3. Combine oranges and coconut.
4. Dice bananas. Place 4 pieces of banana in each serving dish before filling with orange mixture.
5. Garnish each portion with a cherry ring.

FRESH FRUIT CUP
WITH LEMON SHERBET

Yield: 50 portions

Ingredients

PINEAPPLE, FRESH, cut in 1/2-inch cubes	2 quarts
ORANGE SECTIONS	3 cups
BANANAS, diced	3 cups
STRAWBERRIES, cut in half	2 quarts
FRUIT JUICE	3 cups
LEMON SHERBET	2-1/2 to 3 quarts

Procedure

1. Mix fruits together carefully; add fruit juice. Chill.

2. Fill sherbet dishes half full with fruit mixture. Place a No. 20 scoop of sherbet on top.

FRUIT AMBROSIA
WITH COCONUT TOPPING

Yield: 24 portions

Ingredients

PINEAPPLE CHUNKS	1 No. 10 can
PINEAPPLE SYRUP	2 cups
FRUIT COCKTAIL	1 No. 10 can
NONFAT DRY MILK	2 cups
LEMON JUICE	1/2 cup
COCONUT, TOASTED, FLAKED	1 quart

Procedure

1. Drain pineapple; reserve required amount of syrup. Chill syrup.

2. Arrange pineapple and undrained fruit cocktail in serving dishes.

3. Mix nonfat dry milk with well-chilled pineapple syrup. Whip until soft peaks form (3 to 4 minutes). Add lemon juice; continue beating until stiff peaks form (3 to 4 minutes longer).

4. Fold in coconut. Top fruit with coconut topping.

FRESH FRUIT AMBROSIA

Yield: 50 portions

Ingredients

PINEAPPLES, FRESH	4
GRAPEFRUIT	8 medium
ORANGES	12 large
PEARS	3 pounds
APPLES	3 pounds
BANANAS	4 pounds
SUGAR	1 cup
WATER	1 cup
ORANGE JUICE	1 cup
LEMON JUICE	1/4 cup
KIRSCH	1 cup
COCONUT, SHREDDED	1 quart

Procedure

1. Peel and dice pineapples, grapefruit, and oranges. Dice pears and apples; peel and slice bananas.

2. Prepare syrup by combining sugar, water, orange and lemon juice. Stir until sugar is dissolved; add Kirsch.

3. Blend syrup into fruits; chill thoroughly. When serving, mound fruit in dessert or sherbet dish; sprinkle with shredded coconut. Serve very cold.

PEARADISE AMBROSIA

Yield: 50 portions

Ingredients

PINEAPPLE, CRUSHED	1 No. 10 can
COCONUT	1 quart
PEARS, CANNED	50 halves
MARASCHINO CHERRIES	25

Procedure

1. Combine pineapple and coconut; toss until mixed.

2. Place a pear half in a dessert dish, cut side up. Spoon 1/4 cup of the pineapple mixture over the pear. Garnish each portion with half a maraschino cherry.

SPIRITED RAISINS (BASIC RECIPE)

Yield: 24 2-ounce portions

Ingredients

RAISINS, DARK SEEDLESS OR GOLDEN	2 pounds
BRANDY *OR* LIQUEUR	3 cups

Procedure

1. Put raisins into 2 sterilized quart jars.
2. Warm the brandy or liqueur. Do not boil. Pour over raisins. Seal jars.
3. Let stand 24 hours or more, shaking jars occasionally.

Cling Peach Advisory Board

Spirited Fruit

FRUIT COCKTAIL WITH BRANDIED RAISINS

Yield: 1 portion

Ingredients

FRUIT COCKTAIL	3/4 cup
SPIRITED RAISINS (made with brandy)	2 ounces

Procedure

Combine fruit cocktail and brandied raisins. Spoon into serving dish.

SLICED ORANGES WITH RAISINS TEQUILA

Yield: 1 portion

Ingredients

FRESH ORANGE SLICES, sugared	6 to 8
SPIRITED RAISINS (made with Tequila)	2 ounces

Procedure

1. Arrange orange slices in serving dish.
2. Ladle raisins over top.

CHILLED PEARS WITH RAISINS CHERI-SUISSE

Yield: 1 portion

Ingredients

PEAR HALVES, CANNED	2
OR WHOLE FRESH PEAR,	
peeled, poached (with stem)	1
SPIRITED RAISINS (made with Swiss	
Chocolate-Cherry Liqueur)	2 ounces

Procedure

1. Arrange pear halves or poached, whole fresh pear in serving dish.
2. Ladle spirited raisins over fruit.

CHOCOLATE ICE CREAM WITH RAISINS KAHLUA

Yield: 1 portion

Ingredients

CHOCOLATE ICE CREAM	1/6 quart
SPIRITED RAISINS (made with coffee-flavored liqueur)	2 ounces

Procedure
1. Scoop ice cream into serving dish.
2. Ladle spirited raisins over ice cream.

ARANCI CARAMELLIZZATI

Yield: 8 portions

Ingredients

ORANGES, LARGE, SEEDLESS	8
SUGAR	2 cups
WATER	1 cup
GRAND MARNIER OR KIRSCH	as needed

Procedure
1. Peel 4 of the oranges with a vegetable peeler, removing a thin layer of peel with no white portion left on peel. Cut peel in thin strips. Place in boiling water to cover for 5 minutes. Drain.

2. Peel all 8 oranges with a sharp knife removing all white portion. Run knife along each section of orange, but leave the oranges whole and intact.

3. Dissolve sugar in water. Bring to a boil. Add peeled oranges; boil 2 minutes. Lift out oranges; cool.

4. Add drained strips of orange peel to syrup. Cook until they look transparent.

5. Place cold oranges in serving dish. Spoon peel over tops. Add a little Grand Marnier or Kirsch to the syrup. Heat slightly. Pour warm sauce over oranges.

CARAMEL DESSERT ORANGES

Yield: 20 portions

Ingredients

ORANGES, FRUIT TYPE, peeled	20
SUGAR	2 pounds, 10 ounces
WATER, boiling	1 quart
BUTTER	1 tablespoon
CANDIED GINGER, finely chopped	1/4 cup

Procedure

1. Slice oranges into 1/4-inch cartwheels; place in a large shallow pan.

2. Heat and stir sugar in a heavy pan, over medium heat, until just melted.

3. Cool slightly; add boiling water, butter, and ginger. Return to heat, stirring constantly, until smooth. Pour hot liquid over oranges. Chill thoroughly, preferably 24 hours.

4. To serve, place 5 to 6 slices of orange in each dessert dish; top with 2 to 3 tablespoons of Cold Whipped Custard Sauce.*

*See recipe, p. 30.

SHERRIED DESSERT ORANGES

Yield: 20 portions

Ingredients

ORANGES, FRUIT TYPE, peeled	20
ORANGE, FRUIT TYPE, unpeeled	1
LEMON	1
SUGAR	2 cups
SHERRY	3 cups
WATER	2 cups
CINNAMON STICK	1

Procedure

1. Slice peeled oranges into 1/4-inch cartwheels; place in large shallow pan.

2. Slice unpeeled orange and lemon; combine with sugar, sherry, water, and cinnamon. Bring to a boil; cook 5 minutes.

3. Strain hot liquid over sliced oranges. Chill thoroughly, preferably 24 hours.

4. Serve orange slices topped with Cold Whipped Custard Sauce. *(See following recipe)*

COLD WHIPPED CUSTARD SAUCE

Yield: approximately 2 quarts

Ingredients

EGG YOLKS	8 (2/3 cup)
WHOLE EGGS	4
SUGAR	1/2 cup
SALT	1/4 teaspoon
CREAM, LIGHT, scalded	1 quart
VANILLA	1 teaspoon
LEMON PEEL, grated	2 teaspoons
CREAM, HEAVY	2 cups

Procedure

1. Beat yolks and whole eggs together until just blended; add sugar and salt.

2. Add scalded cream, stirring constantly.

3. Cook over simmering water until mixture thickens and coats a spoon. Remove from heat at once to avoid curdling. Add vanilla and lemon peel. Chill.

4. Whip heavy cream; gently fold into custard. Chill thoroughly.

AMERICAN BLUE CHEESE PEARS WITH WINE SAUCE

Yield: 24 portions

Ingredients

BLUE CHEESE	1 pound
MILK	1/3 to 1/2 cup
PEAR HALVES, CANNED, drained	48
PEAR SYRUP	1 quart
DRY SHERRY WINE	3/4 cup

Procedure

1. Crumble cheese, add milk, mixing until well blended. Fill pear cavities with cheese mixture.

2. Place in a shallow baking pan and bake in oven at 400°F. about 10 minutes, or until cheese is melted and pears are thoroughly heated.

3. Combine pear syrup and sherry; heat to boiling.

4. To serve, ladle hot wine sauce into warm serving dishes. Place heated pear halves in sauce allowing two halves per portion.

Poached Pears in Spiced Wine

CODDLED PEARS IN SPICED RUM SAUCE

Yield: 24 portions

Ingredients

SUGAR	1 quart
WATER	3 cups
SALT	1/4 teaspoon
CINNAMON, STICKS (2-inch pieces)	8
CLOVES, WHOLE	1 teaspoon
ALLSPICE, WHOLE	1 teaspoon
GINGER ROOTS, WHOLE	8
PEARS, FRESH (firm, ripe)	24
LIGHT RUM	1-1/2 cups
LEMON ICE *OR* SHERBET	3 quarts

Procedure

1. Combine sugar, water, and salt. Add stick cinnamon. Tie remaining spices in a cheese cloth bag. Add to mixture; bring to boiling point.

2. Peel pears, leaving whole with stems attached. Add pears to hot syrup. Cover; cook slowly, turning occasionally, until tender, about 10 minutes.

3. Remove spice bag. Add rum. Let pears marinate in syrup at least 24 hours.

4. To serve, place a scoop of lemon ice in serving dish. Stand a whole pear upright on sherbet; spoon rum sauce over top.

FRESH NECTARINES WITH SABAYON SAUCE

Yield: 24 portions

Ingredients

NECTARINES, FRESH (firm, ripe)	24
SUGAR	2 cups
WATER	1 quart
ALMOND EXTRACT	1 teaspoon
EGG YOLKS, LARGE	16 (1-1/3 cups)
SUGAR, LIGHT BROWN	6 ounces (1 cup, packed)
ORANGE JUICE *OR* SWEET SHERRY	1-1/3 cups
CREAM, HEAVY	1-1/2 cups

Procedure

1. Quickly dip nectarines in boiling water then in cold water. Slip off skins with sharp knife. Leave nectarines whole or cut in half and remove stones.

2. Combine sugar and water, bring to a boil. Boil 2 to 3 minutes. Add almond extract and nectarines. Cover, cook until nectarines are tender but hold their shape.

3. In top of a double boiler, beat egg yolks until thick and lemon colored. Add brown sugar. Gradually beat in orange juice or sherry.

4. Cook stirring, over hot water (not boiling) until the mixture is very thick.

5. Remove from hot water. Cool.

6. Whip cream; fold into sauce.

7. To serve, place one whole nectarine or 2 halves in serving dish; top with sauce.

DESSERT APHRODITE

Yield: 24 portions

Ingredients

CLING PEACH HALVES, CANNED	24
ALMOND CUSTARD SAUCE	
(See following recipe.)	1-1/2 quarts
ALMOND SLICES	2-1/2 ounces

Procedure

1. Chill peaches thoroughly. Drain.

2. Place a peach half in each serving dish. Add 2 ounces Almond Custard Sauce. Sprinkle with almond slices.

ALMOND CUSTARD SAUCE

Yield: Approximately 1-1/2 quarts

Ingredients

MILK	1-1/2 quarts
CORNSTARCH	3 tablespoons
SUGAR	3/4 cup
SALT	1/2 teaspoon
EGG YOLKS	1/3 cup
VANILLA	1 tablespoon
ALMOND EXTRACT	1/4 teaspoon

Procedure

1. Scald milk.

2. Mix cornstarch, sugar, and salt; stir into hot milk. Cook over hot water 10 to 15 minutes, stirring frequently.

3. Beat egg yolks slightly; add a little of the hot mixture; blend. Combine with remaining hot mixture. Cook 5 minutes longer, stirring constantly.

4. Remove from heat; blend in vanilla and almond extract. Cool quickly. Chill thoroughly before serving.

PEACHES IN LEMON SAUCE

Yield: 24 portions

Ingredients

PEACHES, SLICED, CANNED	1 No. 10 can
EGGS	4
LEMONADE CONCENTRATE	1/2 cup
SYRUP, FROM PEACHES	2 cups
SUGAR	1/4 cup
SALT	1/4 teaspoon
CREAM CHEESE	12 ounces

Procedure

1. Drain peaches; reserve required amount of syrup. Divide peach slices among 24 individual dessert dishes.

2. To make sauce: Beat eggs; add undiluted lemonade concentrate, peach syrup, sugar, and salt. Cook in double boiler or over low heat, stirring constantly, until thick and smooth.

3. Add cream cheese; whip until smooth.

4. Serve sauce warm or cold over the peaches. Accompany with gingersnaps or other crisp cookies, if desired.

STRAWBERRIES AND APRICOTS DEVONSHIRE

Yield: 50 portions

Ingredients

CREAM CHEESE, softened	1-1/2 pounds
SUGAR	1/4 cup
LEMON PEEL, grated	2 teaspoons
LEMON JUICE	1/2 cup
CREAM, HEAVY	3 cups
STRAWBERRIES, WHOLE, FROZEN, partially thawed	6-1/2 pounds
APRICOTS, CANNED HALVES, drained, chilled	2 quarts

Procedure

1. Combine cream cheese, sugar, and lemon peel. Blend in lemon juice, beating until light.

2. Whip cream; fold into cheese mixture.

3. Arrange partially frozen strawberries and chilled apricot halves in serving dishes. Top with sauce.

CHERRIES WITH CURACAO

Yield: Approximately 3 quarts

Ingredients

SUGAR, BROWN, firmly packed	2 cups
CORNSTARCH	1/4 cup
SALT	1/2 teaspoon
ORANGE JUICE	2 cups
BUTTER *OR* MARGARINE	1/4 pound
DARK SWEET CHERRIES, PITTED, drained*	1 No. 10 can
CURACAO	1-1/2 cups

Procedure

1. Mix brown sugar, cornstarch, salt, and orange juice. Cook, stirring until thickened and clear.
2. Add butter and drained cherries; heat.
3. Reduce heat; stir in Curacao.
4. Serve hot over ice cream, chilled vanilla pudding, custard, or slices of angel food cake.

Substitute a No. 10 can of sliced peaches, pear halves cut into thin slices, or purple plums, seeded and quartered, if desired.

BAKED BANANA COCONUT DESSERT

Yield: 24 portions

Ingredients

BANANAS, peeled	24
BUTTER, melted	3/4 cup
LEMON JUICE	3/4 cup
COCONUT, SHREDDED	2 cups

Procedure

1. Cut bananas in 2 pieces; arrange in a buttered baking dish.
2. Brush with melted butter; sprinkle with lemon juice, then with coconut.
3. Bake in oven at 375°F. 15 to 20 minutes or until bananas are tender.
4. Serve warm, with or without cream.

APRICOT FOULE

Yield: Approximately 24 portions

Ingredients

MILK	2 quarts
SUGAR, FINE GRANULATED	12 ounces
CORNSTARCH	4 ounces
SALT	1 teaspoon
EGGS, WHOLE, beaten	6
APRICOTS, DRIED, finely chopped	2 pounds
APRICOT BRANDY	as needed
WHIPPED CREAM	3 cups
NUTMEG	as needed

Procedure

1. Scald milk.

2. Combine sugar, cornstarch, and salt; add to beaten eggs. Gradually add hot milk, mixing well. Cook, stirring constantly, over moderate heat until thickened and smooth. Chill.

3. Soak apricots in brandy until soft.

4. To serve, put a spoonful of apricots into serving dish. Fill with chilled custard mixture. Top with whipped cream. Garnish with pieces of apricot and a dash of nutmeg.

FROZEN CHERRIES AND SOUR CREAM

Yield: 24 portions

Ingredients

CHERRIES, RED, FROZEN	6 pounds
SUGAR	6 tablespoons
SOUR CREAM	1-1/2 cups

Procedure

1. Partially defrost the frozen cherries, but keep very cold.

2. Combine sugar and sour cream.

3. Serve cherries in sherbet dishes topped with the sweetened sour cream.

BANANA LEMON-MACE
PARFAIT

Yield: 32 portions

Ingredients

EGG YOLKS, beaten	4
LEMON JUICE	1/2 cup
LEMON PEEL, grated	1 tablespoon
SUGAR	1/2 cup
MACE	2 teaspoons
EGG WHITES	4
SUGAR	1/2 cup
WHIPPED INSTANT NON-FAT DRY MILK SOLIDS	3 quarts
BANANAS, ripe, sliced	8

Procedure

1. Combine beaten egg yolks, lemon juice, lemon peel, and first amount of sugar. Cook, stirring constantly, over low heat until mixture thickens, 3 to 4 minutes. Add mace; cool.

2. Beat egg whites to soft peaks. Gradually add remaining sugar; beat until stiff peaks form. Fold into cooled mixture.

3. Prepare whipped topping (follow directions on non-fat dry milk package for making whipped topping). Fold into cooled mixture.

4. Fill parfait glasses with alternate layers of dessert mixture and sliced bananas. Garnish with slices of banana and a sprinkling of mace.

WINTER FRUIT KEBAB

Yield: 50 portions

Ingredients

SUGAR	1-1/2 cups
WATER	1-1/2 cups
WHOLE CLOVES	2 teaspoons
WHOLE CINNAMON	2 3-inch sticks
ORANGE JUICE	1 cup
LEMON JUICE	1/4 cup
LEMON PEEL, grated	1 tablespoon
BRANDY *OR* KIRSCH	1-1/2 cups
COINTREAU	1/4 cup
BANANAS	12
PEARS, FRESH	8 pounds
AVOCADOS	12
STRAWBERRIES	2 quarts
ORANGES, cut in half	25

Procedure

1. Combine sugar, water, spices, orange juice, lemon juice, and peel. Bring to a boil; simmer five minutes. Cool. Add brandy or Kirsch and Cointreau.

2. Peel bananas; cut into 1-inch slices. Cut unpeeled pears into thin slices. Peel avocados and cut into small wedges. Wash strawberries.

3. Stir fruit into sauce; marinate for 10 minutes.

4. Just before serving, alternate fruit on 4-inch skewers. Pierce kebab in rounded side of orange half. Or, omit orange and serve flat on plate. Serve with whipped cream dressing, if desired.

CHERRY-BAKED APPLES

Yield: 25 portions

Ingredients

APPLES, (MEDIUM-SIZED), cored	25
MARASCHINO CHERRIES, coarsely chopped	1 cup
WALNUT PIECES	1-1/3 cups
MARASCHINO CHERRY JUICE	1-1/3 cups
SUGAR	1 cup
HONEY	1 cup
WATER, HOT	2 cups

Procedure

1. Arrange apples in baking pans; fill with cherries and walnuts.
2. Combine remaining ingredients; mix well. Pour over apples.
3. Bake in oven at 350°F. 1 hour or until done, basting occasionally with syrup in pan. Serve warm or cool, with cream, if desired.

International Apple Institute

Amber Apples, Cooked in Apple Juice

ROSY CINNAMON APPLES

Yield: 48 Apples

Ingredients

APPLES (80'S)	48
WATER	1 gallon
SUGAR	4 pounds
LEMONS, thinly sliced	4 lemons
CINNAMON CANDY ("red hots")	1 cup
RED FOOD COLORING	1 tablespoon
CREAM CHEESE	3 pounds
MILK *OR* HONEY	as needed
WALNUT HALVES	48

Procedure

1. Core and pare apples.

2. Combine water, sugar, lemon slices, candy, and red food coloring. Bring to a boil, stirring until sugar and candy dissolve.

3. Simmer apples in syrup until tender and red, turning often. Drain; chill.

4; Soften cream cheese with milk or honey. Fill core-space in apples; garnish with walnut half. Serve with a small amount of the syrup as sauce.

Amaretto di Saronno

Meringue-Topped, Flavor-Intense Apple Slices

PEACH DELIGHT

Yield: 25 portions

Ingredients

CRISP MACAROON COOKIES, rolled into fine crumbs	3 quarts
SUGAR	1 cup
DARK RUM	1 cup
YOGHURT, PLAIN	1 quart
PEACHES, CANNED, SLICED, chilled, drained	1 No. 10 can

Procedure

1. Mix crumbs, sugar, and rum.
2. Add yoghurt, mixing gently. Chill.
3. Place a No. 16 scoop of crumb mixture in each serving dish; surround with drained, chilled peach slices.

Cling Peach Advisory Board

Custard Brulee Base for Peachy Topping

STRAWBERRY LADYFINGER DESSERT

Yield: 24 portions

Ingredients

FROZEN STRAWBERRIES, SLICED, thawed	7-1/2 cups
FROZEN ORANGE JUICE CONCENTRATE, thawed	2-1/4 cups
LADYFINGERS (DOUBLE)	100
ORANGE MARMALADE	2 cups
WHIPPED CREAM	to garnish

Procedure

1. Combine strawberries and orange juice concentrate; blend.
2. Arrange 50 ladyfinger halves in bottom of 12-inch by 18-inch shallow pan. Spread with 1/2 cup of the orange marmalade. Pour about 2 cups of the strawberry mixture over ladyfingers.
3. Repeat layers three times. Chill thoroughly.
4. Serve garnished with whipped cream.

HEAVENLY HASH

Yield: 50 portions

Ingredients

PINEAPPLE TIDBITS	1 No. 10 can
MANDARIN ORANGE SECTIONS	4 pounds
RED MARASCHINO CHERRIES, halved	3 pounds
GREEN MARASCHINO CHERRIES, halved	3 pounds
MINIATURE MARSHMALLOWS	6 pounds
FILBERTS, SLICED	1-1/2 pounds
HEAVY CREAM	3 quarts

Procedure

1. Drain fruits.
2. Combine fruits, marshmallows, and filberts.
3. Whip cream; fold into fruit mixture. Chill several hours until thoroughly cold and marshmallows are puffed.
4. Serve in sherbet or parfait dishes or other dessert dishes. Garnish with additional red and green maraschino cherries, whipped cream, orange segments or filberts, as desired.

STRAWBERRY-ORANGE MONT BLANC

Yield: 2 portions

Ingredients

COTTAGE CHEESE	1 cup
SUGAR	1/4 cup
ORANGE PEEL, grated	1 teaspoon
ORANGE JUICE	1 tablespoon
STRAWBERRIES, FROZEN, WHOLE OR SLICED	10 ounces
ORANGES, SLICED OR SECTIONED	2
BRANDY, CURACAO or COINTREAU	2 tablespoons

Procedure

1. Press cottage cheese through sieve; blend with sugar, orange peel and juice.

2. Mound mixture into serving dishes; chill.

3. Drain strawberries, reserving syrup.

4. Add oranges to syrup. Cook in chafing dish for a few minutes. Add strawberries; heat through.

5. Warm brandy; add to fruit mixture, ignite.

6. Spoon fruits over cheese; serve at once.

DUCHESS PEARS

Yield: 50 portions

Ingredients

CHOCOLATE PUDDING OR PIE FILLING, chilled	1 gallon
MERINGUE SHELLS	50
CANNED PEAR HALVES, drained	50
NUTS, coarsely cut	1/2 cup

Procedure

1. If desired, restore gloss and creamy appearance to chilled chocolate filling by beating on mixer for a few turns of the paddle at low speed. Do not overbeat.

2. Fill individual meringue shells allowing approximately 1/3 cup filling per portion. Place drained pear half on top of filling. Finish with a light sprinkling of nuts.

PEARS BAKED IN PINEAPPLE JUICE

Yield: 24 portions

Ingredients

PEARS, BOSC OR BARTLETT	24
SUGAR	1 cup
ORANGE PEEL, grated	2 tablespoons
PINEAPPLE JUICE, CANNED	3 cups
LEMON JUICE	3/4 cup
CINNAMON, 3-inch stick	1
CLOVES, whole (optional)	18

Procedure

1. Peel pears; cut in half; core. Place in baking pan.

2. Spring with sugar and orange peel.

3. Combine canned pineapple juice and lemon juice; pour over pears. Add spice.

4. Cover; bake in oven at 350°F. for 30 minutes, or until pears are tender.

PEACH MACAROONS

Yield: 48 portions

Ingredients

EGG WHITES	4
CORN SYRUP, WHITE	3/4 cup
ALMOND EXTRACT	1-1/2 teaspoons
VANILLA	1-1/2 teaspoons
SUGAR	3/4 cup
BREAD CRUMBS, dry coarse	1-1/2 quarts
PEACH HALVES, LARGE, drained	48

Procedure

1. Beat egg whites until foamy, but not dry. Add corn syrup and flavorings gradually, beating until mixture is shiny and holds stiff peaks.

2. Combine sugar and dry bread crumbs; fold into meringue mixture.

3. Arrange peach halves on a pan 18-inches by 26-inches by 1-inch. Place a No. 30 scoop of macaroon mixture into the cavity of each peach. Bake in oven at 350°F. for 20 minutes.

BROILED FRUIT MEDLEY

Yield: 25 portions

Ingredients

PINEAPPLE SLICES, CANNED, drained	25
CLING PEACH HALVES, CANNED, drained	25
FRUIT JUICE FROM THE DRAINED FRUIT	2 cups
SUGAR, BROWN	1/2 cup
BUTTER	4 ounces

Procedure

1. Arrange fruit in a shallow baking pan. Pour fruit juice around fruit.

2. Sprinkle with sugar; dot with butter. Broil under a low flame until thoroughly heated through and fruit begins to brown.

3. Serve hot topped with ice cream or whipped cream flavored with grated orange peel.

Sauce Arlesienne Adds Savor to Chilled Fruit

HOT FRUIT COMPOTE

Yield: 60 1/2-cup portions

Ingredients

PINEAPPLE TIDBITS, drained	1 No. 10 can
APRICOTS, DRIED, lightly cooked, quartered, drained	2 quarts
SHERRY	3 cups
APPLE SAUCE	1 No. 10 can
SUGAR, BROWN	1 pound
BUTTER	1/4 pound
ALMONDS, sliced	1 cup
MACAROON *OR* COOKIE CRUMBS	2 quarts

Procedure

1. Combine pineapple and apricots. Pour sherry over fruit; let stand 1 hour. Drain, reserving liquid.

2. Divide fruit, placing in two 12-inch by 20-inch by 2-inch pans. Spread half of the apple sauce over each pan.

3. Sprinkle brown sugar over fruit. Divide butter into small dabs; distribute evenly over top. Sprinkle with almonds.

4. Spread macaroon crumbs over top; moisten with liquid (sherry) drained from fruit.

5. Bake in oven at 350°F. for 30 minutes. Serve hot with cream or a Sabayon sauce.

SPICED RHUBARB AND PINEAPPLE COMPOTE

Yield: 24 portions

Ingredients

SUGAR	2 pounds
WATER	3 cups
MACE, GROUND	2 teaspoons
RHUBARB, FRESH, cut in 1-1/2 to 2-inch pieces	2-1/2 quarts
PINEAPPLE WEDGES, FRESH	1-1/2 quarts
FRESH MINT LEAVES	as needed

Procedure

1. Dissolve sugar in water in a 12-inch by 20-inch pan. Add mace.
2. Add rhubarb; cook in oven at 400°F. 15 to 20 minutes or until rhubarb is tender. Cool.
3. Add pineapple. Chill.
4. Serve in iced supreme cups or sherbets. Garnish with mint.

ROYAL ANNE ROSÉ COMPOTE

Yield: 25 portions

Ingredients

ROYAL ANNE CHERRIES, drained	2 cups
PINEAPPLE CHUNKS, drained	2 cups
PEAR HALVES, drained, diced	2 cups
PEACH HALVES, drained, diced	2 cups
MANDARIN ORANGES, drained	2 cups
SYRUP FROM FRUIT*	1-2/3 cups
ROSE WINE	3-1/3 cups

Procedure

1. Drain fruits separately. Remove pits from cherries, if desired. Dice pears and peaches. Combine fruits.
2. Combine syrup from fruit with wine. Pour over fruit. Chill several hours before serving.

*1/3 cup syrup from each fruit.

BAKED FRUIT COMPOTE

Yield: 50 portions

Ingredients

APRICOT HALVES, drained	1 No. 10 can
PEACH HALVES, drained	1 No. 10 can
PURPLE PLUMS, drained	1 No. 10 can
ORANGES, thinly sliced	4
MARASCHINO CHERRIES, halved	1 quart
ORANGE JUICE	3 cups
SUGAR, BROWN	1-1/2 cups (9 ounces)
LEMON PEEL, grated	1 tablespoon
BUTTER *OR* MARGARINE melted	6 ounces
COCONUT	3 cups

Procedure

1. Arrange drained fruit and orange slices in baking pans or individual casseroles. Sprinkle with cherries.

2. Combine orange juice, brown sugar, and lemon peel. Pour over fruits.

3. Drizzle fruits with butter; sprinkle with coconut.

4. Bake in oven at 425°F. 15 minutes.

5. Top with whipped topping or sour cream, if desired.

SPICED HOT FRUIT COMPOTE
(pictured on cover, lower inset)

Yield: Approximately 48 portions

Ingredients

CLING PEACH HALVES (medium)	1 No. 10 can
PEAR HALVES (medium)	1 No. 10 can
MANDARIN ORANGE SECTIONS	2 quarts
CHERRIES, DARK SWEET, pitted, drained	1 No. 10 can
LEMON SLICES, thin, from	1 lemon
CLOVES, WHOLE	2 teaspoons
CINNAMON STICKS, 3-inch	4

Procedure

1. Drain peaches, pears, and orange sections, reserving syrup.

2. Put fruit in shallow pan. Add drained cherries and lemon slices.

3. Measure 1-3/4 quarts of mixed fruit syrup drained from peaches, pears, and oranges. Include a small amount of syrup from cherries, if desired. Add cloves and cinnamon; bring to a boil; cover; simmer 10 minutes.

4. Pour syrup over fruit. Place over low heat or, bake in oven at 350°F. for 20 to 25 minutes or until fruit is heated through. Baste 2 or 3 times while heating. Serve warm.

American Spice Trade Association

Fruit Spiced for Tableside Flaming

FRUITED FLAMBE
(prepared tableside)

Yield: 4 portions

Ingredients

WATER	1/3 cup
SUGAR	1/4 cup
ORANGE JUICE	2 tablespoons
ORANGE PEEL, grated	1/4 teaspoon
LIME PEEL, grated	1/4 teaspoon
BUTTER	1 teaspoon
BANANAS, peeled, whole or cut in halves	4
RUM, LIGHT	2 tablespoons
SOUTHERN COMFORT	1 tablespoon

Procedure

1. Combine water and sugar; boil until syrup thickens. Add orange juice, orange and lime peel. Bring to boiling point; add butter.
2. Add bananas; cook 3 to 4 minutes, basting frequently.
3. Add rum and Southern Comfort; flame.

APRICOTS AU CURACAO

Yield: 1 portion

Ingredients

WHOLE APRICOTS, CANNED	4
SYRUP FROM APRICOTS	1 tablespoon
SUGAR, BROWN (packed measure)	2 tablespoons
BUTTER *OR* MARGARINE	1 teaspoon
CURACAO	1 tablespoon
SOUR CREAM	2 tablespoons

Procedure

1. Put apricots and syrup in a ramekin.
2. Sprinkle with brown sugar; dot with butter.
3. Heat in oven at 300°F. about 20 minutes.
4. Remove from oven. Pour Curacao over apricots. Serve hot. Top with sour cream.

Note

If desired, heat Curacao gently; ignite. Pour, flaming, over apricots.

BAKED BANANAS FLAMBE

Yield: 32 portions (3 pieces each)

Ingredients

BANANAS, firm, ripe	24
LIME JUICE, FRESH	1 cup
SUGAR, BROWN	3 cups
SHERRY WINE	2 cups
CINNAMON, GROUND	1-1/2 teaspoons
NUTMEG, GROUND	1-1/2 teaspoons
CLOVES, GROUND	3/4 teaspoon
ORANGE PEEL, grated	1-1/2 tablespoons
BUTTER *OR* MARGARINE	1/2 cup
BRANDY	1 cup

Procedure

1. Peel bananas. Cut in half crosswise, then lengthwise.

2. Dip each piece in lime juice; place in baking pan. Pour remaining juice over bananas.

3. Combine sugar, sherry, spices, and orange peel; pour over bananas. Dot with butter.

4. Bake in oven at 350°F. 15 to 20 minutes.

5. Just before serving, heat brandy; pour over bananas. Ignite, serve flaming.

ICE CREAM DESSERTS

United Dairy Industry Association

Banana Split Bombe Layers Strawberry, Chocolate, and Banana Ice Cream

55

Sundaes

ICE CREAM has a universal appeal. But in an age when the ubiquitous home freezer has made ice cream a staple, food-service operators can no longer expect a plain, unadorned scoop of ice cream to kindle a high level of interest. Today it takes the addition of a carefully chosen sauce to productively alter the picture and change a too-usual dessert into a glorious sundae. This transformation will happen with the introduction of the suggestions that follow.

SUNDAE IDEAS

With Vanilla Ice Cream:
Apricot syrup, shavings of chocolate
Blueberry sauce
Caramel sauce
Bing cherry sauce with rum or brandy
Minted chocolate sauce
Whole fruit cranberry sauce
Date-nut sauce
Chopped figs with toasted almonds or grated orange peel
Fruit cocktail sauce
Hot fudge sauce, chopped peanuts
Frozen grape juice concentrate
Marron pieces in syrup
Maple syrup with bits of preserved ginger
Hot maple syrup with salted almonds or pecans
Hot mincemeat sauce
Orange marmalade thinned with lemon juice and an orange liqueur
Sliced fresh or frozen peaches
Crushed peanut brittle
Sliced pears and Creme de Menthe
Crushed pineapple and chopped fresh mint

Fresh pineapple and strawberries
Praline crunch
Crushed raspberries or strawberries
Buttered rum sauce (caramel sauce with rum)

With Chocolate Ice Cream:
Butterscotch sauce, salted whole almonds
Chocolate sauce, toasted coconut
Chocolate-peanut butter sauce
Honey-coffee sauce
Rich custard sauce with toasted almonds or crushed pep-
permint candy
Marshmallow creme, shaved chocolate

National Cherry Growers and Industries Foundation

Sundae Splendor with Dark Sweet Cherries

Grated orange peel mixed with sugar
Crushed peppermint stick candy

With Coffee Ice Cream:
Apricot sauce
Chopped chocolate almond bark candy
Custard sauce, shaved chocolate
Fudge sauce, chopped nuts

United Dairy Industry Association

Sophisticated Sundaes

Marshmallow creme, a dab of mint jelly

Brandied hot mincemeat sauce

Sliced peaches and rich custard sauce

Buttered rum sauce (caramel sauce with rum)

With Sherbets:

A cone-shaped scoop of lemon sherbet with Creme de Menthe

Lemon sherbet with pitted dark sweet cherries

Lemon or orange sherbet with diced orange or diced fresh pineapple

Lemon or pineapple sherbet with a splash of brandy

Lime sherbet with pineapple sauce

Orange sherbet with ginger sauce (thinned ginger marmalade, when available)

Orange sherbet with Curacao or other orange liqueur

Orange sherbet and vanilla ice cream with Grand Marnier

Raspberry sherbet with Cassis

Aflame:

Apricots Jubilee with brandy

Cherries Jubilee with rum or brandy

Peaches Jubilee with brandy

Black cherries and sliced peaches with brandy

Fruit cocktail with rum or brandy

Mincemeat with brandy

Strawberries with Kirsch

Purple plums with brandy

Brandied chocolate sauce

Parfaits

THE AMERICAN INTERPRETATION of a parfait usually combines one or more flavors of ice cream (or an ice cream and a sherbet) layered in tall, slender serving dishes with a fruit, a syrup, or a sauce and/or other popular trimmings. The dessert is usually completed with whipped cream or topping and a garnish.

Try these sauces and other parfait ingredients:

Chocolate sauce and toasted, slivered almonds

Chocolate sauce and crushed peppermint candy

Chocolate sauce, chopped maraschino cherries, and rum

Fudge sauce (good between layers of vanilla and pistachio ice cream)

Apricot jam with Kirsch

Sliced preserved marrons in syrup

Crushed sweetened strawberries (a popular choice with vanilla and strawberry ice cream)

Sliced strawberries with orange juice and a bit of grated orange peel

Orange marmalade or sliced preserved kumquats laced with Curacao (nice with a combination of vanilla ice cream and orange sherbet)

Nesserode sauce

Chopped dates, pecans, and honey (combines well with butter pecan ice cream)

Macaroon crumbs moistened with rum or Amaretto di Saronno

Fruit cake crumbs or crumbled fig cookies sprinkled with sherry or brandy (try layering with vanilla and coffee ice cream)

Creme de Menthe

Tia Maria

Creme de Cacao

Sunkist Growers

Fruit-Layered Parfait

Ice Cream Pies

THE BEST FEATURES of two popular desserts—ice cream and pie—combine to make novel ice cream pies. In their four versions—plain, garnished, meringue topped (Alaska), or sauced (Sundae Pie)—these desserts are as versatile as they are popular.

Variety is enhanced by rotating ice cream's numerous flavors, combinations of flavors, and added particles of fruit and/or nuts, ripples of syrup, and bits of crushed candy. Premise-made crumb crusts lend themselves to a variety of adaptations; plain crumb crusts are available ready-to-use. There are any number of appropriate toppings and garnishes for ice cream pies:

Ice Cream Flavor(s)	*Crust(s) and Garnish(es)*
Coffee	Date-nut crust; shaved Brazil nut garnish
Strawberry	Coconut crust; whole strawberry garnish
Vanilla	Harlequin crust; crust crumb garnish
	Peanut butter crust; crushed peanut brittle garnish
Butter Pecan	Semi-sweet crust; whipped cream border and maraschino cherry garnish
Cherry	Bittersweet crust; drizzles of chocolate sauce on top
Chocolate	Nutty crust; whipped cream and toasted almonds on top
Rum	Raisin crust; chopped nut garnish
Peach	Spiced crust; crust crumb garnish or decorative border
Vanilla/Orange Sherbet (two layer pie)	Orange crust; shaved chocolate garnish

To make ice cream pie, fill a well-chilled baked or unbaked crumb crust with slightly softened ice cream that is comple-

mentary to the chosen crust in color and flavor. Choose a single flavor of ice cream, or use two or three flavors spooned or spaced alternately into the crust to give a marbled effect. Freeze the filled crust for several hours, until firm, or overnight. For added flourish, spread with whipped cream. Additional garnish ideas follow:

Crumbs reserved from crust

Plain, toasted, or tinted shredded coconut

Shaved chocolate

Chopped nuts

A sprinkling of spice

Whole, uncapped strawberries, or strawberry slices arranged fan-wise

Maraschino cherries

Sliced banana

Sprigs of mint

Crushed peanut brittle

Crushed peppermint stick candy

Advisory Council for Jams, Jellies, and Preserves

Frozen Grape Pie

For Alaska pie, fill a crust as for ice cream pie. Spread meringue over ice cream, sealing meringue carefully to edge of crust. Sprinkle meringue coating lightly with sugar and freeze pie. Keep in freezer storage until serving time. Bake quickly in oven at 500° F. until meringue is delicately browned. Serve at once, with or without a sauce.

An ice cream pie becomes Sundae Pie when topped by or accompanied by one of the following sauces:

Chocolate
Butterscotch
Hot fudge
Marshmallow cream
Crushed pineapple
Whole cranberry
Red or dark sweet cherry
Strawberry
Raspberry
Melba
Apricot
Sliced peach

To make Sundae Pie, fill a crust as for ice cream pie and freeze. Serve in wedges with a Sundae sauce. Possible combinations of ice cream flavors and Sundae sauces follow:

Ice Cream Flavor(s)	Crust(s) and Sauce(s)
Peach	Coconut crust; melba sauce
Vanilla	Basic crust; strawberry sauce (try a garnish of sliced bananas)
	Spicy crust; sliced peach sauce
Mint	Bittersweet crust; hot fudge sauce
Coffee	Nutty crust; butterscotch sauce
Chocolate	Peanut butter crust; marshmallow cream on top
Rum	Basic crust; bing cherry sauce
Vanilla	Raisin crust; mincemeat sauce

Finally, sauces that lend themselves to flaming for dramatic ice cream pie service include:

Brandied bing cherries
Brandied cherries and sliced peaches
Fruit cocktail with rum
Apricot with Kirsch
Brandied mincemeat

GRAHAM CRACKER CRUSTS
(Basic Recipe)

Yield: Six 9-inch

Ingredients

GRAHAM CRACKER CRUMBS	2-1/4 pounds
BUTTER *OR* MARGARINE (softened to room temperature)	1 pound
SUGAR	1 pound

Procedure

1. Combine crumbs, softened butter, and sugar; blend thoroughly on mixer, using paddle at low speed for 3 minutes.

2. Divide mixture into 9-inch pie plates; press firmly against bottom and sides of plate using an 8-inch pie plate to press crumbs into shape.

3. For unbaked crusts: Chill thoroughly before using. For baked crusts: Bake 8 minutes in oven at 375°F.

GRAHAM CRACKER CRUST VARIATIONS

Follow basic recipe above using 1 pound softened butter and 1 pound sugar. To the suggested amount of graham cracker crumb, sugar, and butter mixture, add ingredients in the amounts shown in the chart below.

		Additions to Basic Recipe for Graham Cracker Crusts	
Crust	Graham Cracker Crumb	Add to Crumbs, Butter and Sugar	Suggested Fillings
Bittersweet	2-1/4 pounds	12 ounces unsweetened chocolate, melted	Coffee, Vanilla, or Peppermint Stick ice cream
Coconut	1-3/4 pounds	2 cups flaked coconut	Apricot, Lemon or Pumpkin Chiffon; Strawberry ice cream
Date-Nut	1-3/4 pounds	2 cups dates, finely chopped 2 cups nuts, finely chopped	Butterscotch Cream; Caramel Ripple ice cream
Harlequin	2-1/4 pounds	9 ounces candy sprinkles	Vanilla ice cream; Strawberry Chiffon
Nutty	2 pounds	3 cups nuts, finely chopped	Chocolate ice cream; Prune or Chocolate Chiffon

Orange	2-1/4 pounds	1/2 cup orange rind, grated	Orange Chiffon; Orange Parfait; Coconut Cream
Peanut Butter	2-1/4 pounds	Use 1/2 pound butter only. Add 1-1/4 cups peanut butter, creamy style	Chocolate Chiffon; Banana Cream; Fudge Ripple ice cream
Raisin	2 pounds	3 cups raisins, finely chopped	Cheese Cake; Eggnog Chiffon; Rum ice cream
Semi-sweet	2 pounds	3 cups semi-sweet chocolate pieces	Butter Pecan ice cream; Vanilla and Chocolate Cream (layered or marbled)
Spiced	2-1/4 pounds	Use brown sugar. Add 2 tablespoons cinnamon	Cheese Cake; Peach ice cream; Mincemeat Chiffon; Pumpkin Chiffon

Ice Cream Balls

TO CREATE these favorites of dessert fanciers, shape ice cream into balls; roll the balls in one of the following coatings; then complete your presentation with a complementary sauce. Choose among those listed below, or create your own:

Coatings:
Plain, toasted, or tinted shredded coconut
Chopped walnuts, pecans, almonds, peanuts
Shaved chocolate
Crushed peppermint candy
Crushed peanut brittle

Companionable Sauces:
Chocolate sauce
Hot fudge sauce

California Strawberry Advisory Board

Coconut Ice Cream Balls

68

Butterscotch sauce
Brandy custard sauce
Rum-butter sauce
Crushed pineapple sauce
Sliced peach sauce
Sliced or crushed strawberries
Red raspberry sauce

A Sampling of Combinations:
Coconut snowball with fudge sauce or sliced peach sauce
Toasted almond ice cream ball with hot butterscotch sauce
Chopped peanut ice cream ball with chocolate sauce
Ice cream ball wrapped in shaved chocolate with brandy
    custard sauce
Coconut ice cream ball (tinted a delicate pink) with minted
    pineapple sauce

United Dairy Industry Association

Walnut-Coated Ice Cream Balls with Chocolate Sauce

Festive
Ice Cream Desserts

APPEALING SPECIALTIES can be created by combining ice cream flavors or by incorporating baked goods in a festive way.

Try offering a cluster of small scoops of ice cream in different flavors and colors. Or, offer two flavors of ice cream, or an ice cream and a sherbet, dipped together so they share the same scoop. For example, try chocolate ice cream with pistachio, butter pecan, or peppermint stick; vanilla ice cream with lemon or raspberry sherbet.

Present ice cream with a cookie or two, or a small piece of cake. Brownies and chocolate chip cookies enhance several kinds of ice cream. Sugar cookies go well with everything. Rolled cookies, plain or with ends dipped in a chocolate glaze, are another treat. Miniature rolled cookies make a fetching garnish for a parfait. Tiny cup cakes or small, square or diamond-shaped pieces cut from an iced sheet cake update "ice cream and cake," a long-time favorite.

The popular a la mode approach refers to pie, of course; but also to portions of cake, warm deep-dish pies and cobblers, simple puddings, dessert waffles, brownies, and other bar cookies. Adding a sauce provides a luxurious touch to many desserts served a la mode. Brownies and cake squares topped with ice cream are far more inviting when teamed with a sauce. The same is true of dessert waffles and certain fruit pies.

- Chocolate brownies made with dates and walnuts, topped with a scoop of vanilla ice cream, and a swirl of brandied fudge sauce
- Crisp waffles with cherry ice cream and warm blueberry or other fruit sauce
- Angel food cake, strawberry or vanilla ice cream, and sliced strawberry sauce
- Cherry pie a la mode with an eye-catching bonus of red cherry sauce

Feature ice cream in some type of shell. In addition to pie shells, the possibilities include hollowed-out halves of pineapple, oranges, lemons, or coconut shells. On a more traditional note are eclair and cream puff shells—the classic frozen eclair comes with chocolate glaze. Cream puff shells permit a greater latitude. Made portion-size, they can be filled with any desired flavor of ice cream and served with a companionable sauce. A cluster of three small puff shells makes an attractive offering when filled with vanilla ice cream and topped with chocolate, caramel or Melba sauce. Meringue shells or frozen dessert shells can be fashioned in a choice of shapes—round, oval, heart-shaped, or square—and can be served in their natural white color or tinted to a delicate shade. Like so many ice cream offerings, those served in shells are enormously enhanced by a flourish of sauce. Ice cream served in sponge cake shells, individual or layer cake size, can be presented with crushed berries or other favorite sauce. Similarly, a lace cookie that has been molded, while still warm, in the shape of a cup can be fitted with ice cream and presented with a garnish or sauce as desired. Other shell inspirations include tart shells (see Ice Cream Pies) and Chocolate sundae shells (see recipe and picture pages 90-91.)

Offer ice cream made up as a form.

This dessert is usually served to several people, such as a table of eight or ten.

- *Baked Alaska* consists of a thick mound or brick of firmly frozen ice cream on a thin layer of cake, the whole completely covered with meringue, and quickly baked. A spectacular dessert when served flaming or with a flaming sauce, Baked Alaska can also be constructed as an individual offering.

- *Ice cream bombes* are prepared by lining large molds with layers of ice cream having harmonious flavors and a pleasing contrast of colors. At least two kinds of ice cream should be used, often more. (See photos, pages 55, 88, and 98, for sample arrangements of ice cream layers.)

- *Ice cream rolls* may be prepared by spreading sheets of chocolate or vanilla sponge cake with slightly softened ice cream, then rolling up sheets as for a jelly roll. For variety, drizzle thick chocolate or butterscotch sauce over the ice cream and sprinkle with nuts before rolling. Or spread the ice cream with jelly or jam. Another suggestion: try spreading the surface of the finished roll with a glaze and adding a sprinkling of nuts.

- *Ice cream cakes* are constructed by combining ice cream and cake in a cake-shaped form, with cake or cookies around the outside. The ice cream and cake can also be arranged in alternate layers. For a simple version, line a spring-form pan or a flat mold with foil (heart-shaped molds are a popular choice); let the foil extend over the edge of the pan to facilitate removing the finished dessert. Stand lady fingers, thin slices of jelly roll, or shortbread cookies around the edge of the mold. Fill with ice cream and freeze.

- *Layered ice cream cakes* offer unusual opportunities for originality. Use of several flavors of ice cream, together with liqueurs, fresh fruits, preserves, nuts, macaroon crumbs, and other toppings between the layers of ice cream and cake. To prepare, line a loaf pan or spring-form pan with foil; arrange layers of ice cream and thin layers of cake in the pan, beginning with cake and ending with ice cream; freeze. Spread top and sides with whipped cream; decorate with additional whipped cream; garnish as desired.

- *Schaum torte* is made by using ice cream as a filling between baked round or square layers of firm meringue, this layered confection permits employing more than one flavor and color of ice cream. Add a decorative finishing touch of whipped cream. Schaum tortes are traditionally served with a sauce.

STRAWBERRY ALASKA JUBILEE

Yield: One Alaska, approximately 12 inches by 16 inches

Ingredients
FROZEN SPONGE CAKE
  (sheet form)   1 cake, approximately
                       12 inches by 16 inches
                       by 1 inch

STRAWBERRY ICE CREAM,
  slightly softened   3 quarts
WHIPPED TOPPING   2 quarts
FROZEN WHOLE STRAWBERRIES,
  halved   as needed

Procedure
1. If cake, as purchased, is more than one inch high, split in half horizontally while still frozen and use only half thickness.
2. Spread strawberry ice cream evenly over cake, bringing to edge of cake on all sides.
3. Cover top and sides with whipped topping.
4. Place dessert in freezer. Cut as needed; garnish with frozen strawberry halves. Serve with Flaming Strawberry Sauce, following recipe.

FLAMING STRAWBERRY SAUCE

Yield: 2 cups

Ingredients
FROZEN STRAWBERRIES IN SYRUP   2 cups
CORNSTARCH   2 tablespoons
BRANDY, warm   3 tablespoons

Procedure
1. Thaw strawberries; drain, reserving syrup.
2. Blend cornstarch and syrup. Cook over medium heat until thickened and clear. Remove from heat; stir in strawberries.
3. Pour sauce into chafing dish. Just before serving, add warm brandy. Without stirring, ignite sauce. Ladle flaming sauce over cake.

CALIFORNIA STRAWBERRY BAKED ALASKA

Yield: 48 to 54 slices

Ingredients

SPONGE CAKE	3 sheets (13 inches by 9-1/2 inches by 2 inches)
EGG WHITES	1 pound, 12 ounces
SALT	2 teaspoons
VANILLA	2 teaspoons
SUGAR	1 pound, 12 ounces
STRAWBERRY ICE CREAM	6 one-quart bricks
STRAWBERRIES, FROZEN	5 pounds

Procedure

1. Cut each sheet of sponge cake in half, making 6 pieces. Place on boards covered with brown paper.

2. With sharp knife, cut about 1/2 inch deep around each cake, 1 inch from the edge. Hollow out some of the cake from center, leaving the 1 inch rim around the cakes.

3. Beat egg whites, salt, and vanilla to a stiff foam. Add sugar gradually. Beat until mixture piles up well in the bowl and the sugar is dissolved.

4. Place a solidly frozen brick of ice cream in hollowed-out center of each cake.

5. Cover cake and ice cream completely with meringue. Brown meringue in oven at 450°F.

6. For banquet service, slip from paper onto oblong platters. Slice each cake into 8 or 9 portions at table.

7. Pass bowls of just-thawed frozen strawberries to be ladled over each portion.

INDIVIDUAL BAKED CHERRY ALASKA

Yield: 16 portions

Ingredients

EGG WHITES	12 ounces
SALT	1/2 teaspoon
VANILLA	1/2 teaspoon
SUGAR	12 ounces
WHITE *OR* YELLOW SHEET CAKE,	
4-inch by 2-inch pieces	16
CHERRY ICE CREAM	2 1/2-gallon cartons

Procedure

1. Beat egg whites, salt, and vanilla to a stiff foam. Add sugar gradually. Beat until mixture piles up well in the bowl and the sugar is dissolved.

2. Place pieces of cake on boards covered with brown paper.

3. Cut slices of solidly frozen ice cream slightly smaller than pieces of cake. Place ice cream on cake.

4. Quickly spread meringue, covering cake and ice cream completely. Brown meringue in oven at 450°F. about 3 minutes.

5. Serve with Cherry Sauce, following recipe.

CHERRY SAUCE

Yield: 16 portions

Ingredients

SOUR RED CHERRIES, frozen,	
thawed, drained	2-1/2 cups
SUGAR	1/2 cup
CORNSTARCH	2 tablespoons
SALT	1/8 teaspoon
CHERRY JUICE AND WATER	
to equal	1-1/2 cups
BUTTER	1 tablespoon

Procedure

1. Drain sufficient cherries to yield 2-1/2 cups fruit, reserving juice.

2. Measure cherry juice; add water, if necessary, to equal 1-1/2 cups.

3. Mix sugar, cornstarch, and salt. Stir in cherry juice. Cook, stirring until thickened and clear.

4. Add cherries and butter. Serve warm or cold.

BAKED ALASKA

Yield: 10 portions

Ingredients

EGG WHITES	6 (3/4 cup)
CREAM OF TARTAR	1/4 teaspoon
SALT	1/4 teaspoon
SUGAR	1 cup (7 ounces)
VANILLA	1-1/2 teaspoons
SPONGE CAKE OR GENOISE	1 10-inch layer
ICE CREAM, firmly frozen	1-1/2 quarts
CANDIED CHERRIES	as needed

Procedure

1. For meringue, beat egg whites with cream of tartar and salt until foamy throughout. Add sugar gradually, beating until stiff peaks form. Add vanilla.

2. Cover a thick wooden board with heavy brown paper. Place cake round on paper. Cover with firm ice cream, allowing cake to extend 1/2 inch beyond ice cream all around.

3. Cover ice cream and cake with a thick layer of meringue. Decorate with rosettes of meringue and candied cherries.

4. Bake in oven at 450°F. until meringue is delicately browned.

5. Remove to chilled platter. Serve at once.

PEACH MELBA

Yield: 1 portion

Ingredients

ICE CREAM, VANILLA	No. 12 scoop
PEACH HALF	1
MELBA SAUCE	1 ounce
WHIPPED CREAM	as needed
MARASCHINO CHERRY	1

Procedure

1. Place ice cream in a supreme cup; top with peach half.

2. Pour Melba sauce over peach. Garnish with whipped cream and cherry.

FLAMING FROZEN ECLAIR

Yield: 1 dessert

Ingredients

ECLAIR SHELL	1
PEACH ICE CREAM	2 No. 30 scoops
WHIPPED CREAM (dispenser)	as needed
RASPBERRIES, FROZEN, thawed	2 ounces

Procedure

1. Remove top from eclair shell; hollow out shell.

2. Place ice cream firmly into eclair shell. Circle ice cream with whipped cream. Replace top of eclair shell.

3. Ladle raspberries, flaming, over entire dessert. (Flambe with Framboise, Kirsch, or lemon extract.)

United Dairy Industry Association

Lime-Layered Alaska Pie

BANANAS PATRICIA

Yield: 24 portions

Ingredients

CHOCOLATE, UNSWEETENED	4 ounces
BUTTER *OR* MARGARINE	2 ounces
SUGAR	2 cups
CORNSTARCH	4 teaspoons
SALT	1/4 teaspoon
WATER	1-1/3 cups
CORN SYRUP, LIGHT	1 cup
VANILLA	4 teaspoons
VANILLA ICE CREAM	3 to 4 quarts
BANANAS, firm, ripe	12

Procedure

1. Melt chocolate and butter over hot water.

2. Combine sugar, cornstarch, salt, and water; add to chocolate mixture. Blend in syrup.

3. Stir over low heat until mixture comes to a boil. Cook, stirring, for 3 to 4 minutes. Remove from heat; add vanilla. Cool.

4. Put a scoop of ice cream in serving dish; top with diagonal slices of banana, cut 1/2-inch thick. Ladle 1 ounce chocolate sauce over top.

FROSTY WHIP

Yield: 1 portion

Ingredients

APPLE JUICE, chilled	1 cup
VANILLA ICE CREAM	1 No. 12 scoop
MARASCHINO CHERRIES, chopped	1 tablespoon
NUTMEG (optional)	Dash

Procedure

1. Put apple juice in blender or electric fountain mixer. Add ice cream; mix until frothy.

2. Stir in cherries. Pour into tall glass. Sprinkle with nutmeg, if desired.

BRANDY GLO

Yield: 1 portion

Ingredients
ICE CREAM, RUM FLAVOR (WITH BRAZIL NUTS)	2 No. 16 scoops
COCONUT, SHREDDED	1/4 cup
WHITE CREME DE CACAO	1 tablespoon
BRANDY	1 tablespoon

Procedure
1. Roll ice cream in coconut; place in brandy snifter.
2. Flame white creme de cacao and brandy; pour over ice cream.

Fruit in Sherbet-lined Champagne Glasses (described under spirited fruit desserts, p. 20)

Sunkist Growers, Inc.

FRUIT PARFAITS

Yield: 24 8-ounce parfaits

Ingredients

RED RASPBERRIES, frozen	2 pounds (3-3/4 cups)
NECTARINES OR PEACHES, fresh	6 pounds
SUGAR	2 cups
ICE CREAM, VANILLA	6 quarts
CREAM, HEAVY	2 cups
SUGAR	1/2 cup

Procedure

1. Partially thaw raspberries.
2. Peel and slice nectarines or peaches; add sugar. Mix lightly with raspberries; chill.
3. To serve: Scoop ice cream into bottom of each large parfait glass. Cover generously with fruit; repeat layers. Pour a few spoonfuls of juice from the fruit over each parfait.
4. Whip cream; blend in sugar. Top each parfait with whipped cream.

PARTY CLOWN

Yield: 1 portion

Ingredients

COCONUT, SHREDDED MOIST	1/4 cup
ICE CREAM *OR* SHERBET	1 scoop
SEMI-SWEET CHOCOLATE PIECES	3
PAPER CLOWN HEAD (PURCHASED)	1

Procedure

1. Spread coconut in a circle on dessert plate; place scoop of ice cream or sherbet in center.
2. Arrange chocolate pieces in row down side of ice cream ball for buttons. Top ice cream with clown head.

Chocolate-Vanilla Parfait

PEARWICH

Yield: 1 portion

Ingredients

SOFT-SERVE ICE CREAM	3 ounces
GREEN MINTED PEARS* *OR*	
RED CINNAMON PEARS**	2 halves

Procedure

1. Dispense a ribbon of soft-serve ice cream into serving dish.

2. Place a tinted pear half on either side of ice cream, setting pears on sides. Press gently into the ice cream to create a sandwich effect.

*To prepare green minted pears, drain one No. 10 can pear halves. Measure syrup. For each cup syrup, use 1/2 teaspoon mint extract and 1/2 teaspoon green fruit coloring. Add green coloring to syrup; bring to a boil. Remove from heat; add mint extract. Pour over pears, covering completely. Refrigerate overnight.

**To prepare Red Cinnamon Pears, drain one No. 10 can pear halves. Measure syrup. For each cup syrup, add 1 stick cinnamon and 1 teaspoon red coloring; bring to a boil. Pour over pears, covering completely. Cool. Remove cinnamon; refrigerate overnight.

CORN FLAKE RING DESSERT

Yield: 12 portions

Ingredients

MOLASSES, DARK	1/2 cup
SUGAR	1/4 cup
BUTTER	1 tablespoon
	(rounded measure)
CORN FLAKES	1-1/2 quarts
ICE CREAM, VANILLA	1-1/2 quarts
CARAMEL SAUCE, thin	3 cups

Procedure

1. Combine molasses and sugar; boil until syrup forms a firm ball in cold water (248°F.).

2. Remove from heat; add butter. Stir until butter is melted. Pour over corn flakes, mixing gently but thoroughly.

3. Turn into a well-buttered 1-1/2 quart ring mold; chill.

4. Unmold; fill center of ring with No. 10 scoops of ice cream. Serve with a thin caramel sauce.

KONA

Yield: 1 portion

Ingredients

COCONUT ICE CREAM	1 No. 12 scoop
BANANA	1/2
PINEAPPLE	1 slice
APRICOT PRESERVES	2 tablespoons
RUM	1-1/2 ounces

Procedure

1. Place ice cream in abalone shell.

2. Slice banana; cut pineapple slice into halves. Arrange fruit around ice cream.

3. Blend apricot preserves with a small amount of the rum, thinning to sauce consistency. Spoon over ice cream.

4. Warm remaining rum slightly. Ignite; pour over top of dessert.

California Strawberry Advisory Board

Cream Puff Presentation with Ice Cream and Berries

PEACH CRISPIES

Yield: 24 portions

Ingredients

CLING PEACHES, HALVES, (24 TO 30 COUNT) chilled	1 No. 10 can
SUGAR, BROWN	1-1/2 pounds
FLOUR	2 tablespoons
WATER	1/2 cup
BUTTER *OR* MARGARINE	1/2 pound
OVEN-TOASTED RICE CEREAL	1 gallon
VANILLA ICE CREAM	1 gallon

Procedure

1. Drain peach halves.

2. Combine brown sugar, flour, water, and butter. Bring to boil, stirring until butter is melted. Boil 1 minute, no longer.

3. Remove from heat; pour at once over rice cereal, tossing gently to coat well.

4. Turn into well greased 18-inch by 12-inch by 1-inch bun pan. Spread evenly. Cool.

5. Cut into 24 squares; top each square with a No. 12 scoop of ice cream and a chilled peach half.

United Dairy Industry Association

Ice Cream Contrast for Warm Baked Dessert

ALMOND DESSERT EXTRAORDINAIRE

Yield: 24 (3-1/2-inch)

Ingredients

ALMONDS, SLICED NATURAL	2-1/2 cups (12 ounces)
EGG WHITES	2 cups
CREAM OF TARTAR	1 tablespoon
SALT	1-1/2 teaspoons
CONFECTIONERS' SUGAR, sifted	3 pounds
ALMOND EXTRACT	1/4 teaspoon
COFFEE ICE CREAM	3 quarts
CHOCOLATE SAUCE	4-1/2 cups

Procedure

1. Lightly toast almonds. Chop 2 cups coarsely; reserve remainder for garnish.

2. Beat egg whites, cream of tartar, and salt together until stiff. Beat in half of the sugar, continuing to beat until very stiff. Add almond extract.

3. Combine remaining sugar with chopped almonds; fold into meringue.

4. With pastry bag and No. 8 star tip (slightly spread) form nests on paper-lined or greased and floured 26-inch by 18-inch by 1-inch pan.

5. Bake in oven at 200°F. until shells loosen easily from pan, about 1 hour. Cool.

6. Fill meringues with ice cream. Top with chocolate sauce. Garnish with reserved toasted almonds.

CAKE CRUNCHIES
(for ice cream balls)

Yield: Topping for 16 balls

Ingredients

CORN SYRUP	1 cup
SUGAR, BROWN	1 cup
MOLASSES	2 tablespoons
WATER	1/2 cup
BUTTER	2 tablespoons
CAKE, 1/4 inch cubes, toasted	2 quarts

Procedure

1. Combine syrup, brown sugar, molasses, and water. Boil slowly until mixture reaches 238°F. or until a small amount of syrup forms a soft ball in cold water.

2. Add butter and toasted cake cubes. Mix well. Pour into a greased pan. Cool.

3. Break into pieces.

4. Use to coat ice cream balls.

RIPPLED ICE CREAM MOLDS

Yield: 32 4-ounce portions

Ingredients

SHERBET, LIME, ORANGE OR LEMON	2 quarts
VANILLA ICE CREAM	2 quarts
CREAM, HEAVY	2 cups
SUGAR	1/2 cup
GRAPES, GREEN, quartered	1 cup

Procedure

1. Spoon alternate layers of sherbet and ice cream into molds. Pack firmly; cover; freeze.

2. Whip cream until it holds a peak; blend in sugar. Fold grapes into cream; chill.

3. To serve: Dip bottom of molds quickly into warm water; loosen ice cream with spatula. Invert on chilled serving plates. Top with cream and grape mixture.

Strawberry Bombe

BOMBE HELENE

Yield: 1 2-quart mold (16 to 18 portions)

Ingredients

CHOCOLATE ICE CREAM	1 quart
VANILLA ICE CREAM	1 quart
PEAR HALVES, CANNED	16 to 18
CHOCOLATE SAUCE	2 cups
KIRSCH	1-1/2 ounces
WHITE CREME DE MENTHE	1 ounce

Procedure

1. Line a shallow, oval 2-quart mold with chocolate ice cream, pressing ice cream to cover entire surface of mold. Freeze until firm.

2. Fill center of mold with vanilla ice cream. Pack firmly; return to freezer until well frozen.

3. Unmold; arrange pear halves around base of ice cream, standing them upright against the sides. Decorate top with additional sliced pears.

4. Combine chocolate sauce, Kirsch, and Creme de Menthe; blend well. Serve sauce with portions of the ice cream bombe.

INDIVIDUAL MERINGUE SHELLS

Yield: 6 dozen

Ingredients

EGG WHITES	3 cups
CREAM OF TARTAR	1 tablespoon
SUGAR	1-1/2 quarts

Procedure

1. Beat egg whites until foamy throughout. Add cream of tartar and beat until stiff.

2. Add sugar, 2 tablespoons at a time, beating after each addition until sugar is blended. Continue beating until meringue will stand in very stiff peaks.

3. Line baking sheets with unglazed paper. With a spoon or pastry tube, shape meringues in mounds, allowing 1/3 cup (No. 12 scoop) for each shell. With a spoon make a depression in the center of each.

4. Bake in oven at 275°F. 45 to 50 minutes. Cool; remove from paper.

CHOCOLATE SUNDAE SHELLS
(see picture, opposite)

Yield: 24 shells

Ingredients

PAPER BAKING CUPS	24
SEMI-SWEET CHOCOLATE PIECES	1-1/2 pounds
BUTTER	4 ounces
NUTS, finely chopped	1 cup

Procedure

1. Place baking cups in muffin pans.
2. Combine chocolate pieces and butter; melt over low heat. Stir in nuts.
3. Working quickly, spoon mixture into paper cups; spread to line cups.
4. Chill until firm.
5. To serve, peel off paper cup; fill chocolate cup with ice cream. Serve with sauce, if desired.

Suggested ice cream and sauce combinations:

Ice Cream flavor(s)	Sauce(s)
Butter pecan	Red raspberries in syrup
Cherry	Chocolate sauce
Chocolate	Crushed peppermint stick candy and marshmallow creme
Coffee	Maple syrup
Coffee	Kahlua and chocolate topping
Maple	Creme de Menthe
Mint	Chocolate sauce
Peach	Caramel sauce and toasted almonds
Pistachio	Sweetened strawberries
Pistachio	Sweetened sliced peaches
Strawberry	Lemon pie filling
Vanilla	Chopped pears and chocolate sauce
Vanilla	Peanut butter combined with butterscotch topping

Chocolate Sundae Shells (recipe, p. 90)

Other
Frozen Desserts

FROZEN SPICED FESTIVAL PUDDING

Yield: 30 portions

Ingredients

VANILLA ICE CREAM	3 quarts
CARDAMON, GROUND	3/4 teaspoon
GINGER, GROUND	3/4 teaspoon
NUTMEG, GROUND	3/4 teaspoon
CREAM, HEAVY	3 cups
MIXED GLACE FRUITS	3 cups
CREAM, HEAVY	1-1/2 cups
SUGAR	3 tablespoons

Procedure

1. Let ice cream stand until soft enough to blend with whipped cream and fruit.

2. Add spices to first amount of heavy cream; whip until stiff. Fold whipped cream and glace fruit into ice cream. Turn into individual molds (2/3-cup) or 5 1-quart pudding molds. Place in freezer for 24 hours.

3. Unmold by dipping quickly in warm water. Turn out onto serving plates; return to freezer.

4. Whip remaining cream with sugar. Garnish molds; return to freezer until ready to serve.

FROZEN MOCHA CREAM

Yield: 35 1/2-cup portions

Ingredients

WHIP DESSERT MIX, CHOCOLATE	15 ounces
SUGAR	3/4 cup
INSTANT COFFEE	1/4 cup
WATER, cold	1 quart
SOUR CREAM	1 quart

Procedure

1. Combine dessert mix, sugar, coffee powder, and cold water in mixer bowl.

2. Blend thoroughly at low speed. Whip at high speed 5 minutes or until light and fluffy.

3. Fold in sour cream.

4. Freeze in shallow pans or small dishes at least 4 hours. (Or chill 2 hours for unfrozen dessert.)

5. Garnish with chocolate curls, if desired.

United Dairy Industry Association

Fudge Swirls on Ice Cream Sundae Pie

MERINGUE VELVET

Yield: 6 quarts

Ingredients

CANDIED FRUIT, chopped or diced	2 cups
MARASCHINO LIQUEUR	1 cup
SUGAR, GRANULATED	3-1/3 cups
WATER	1 cup
EGG WHITES, stiffly beaten	12 (1-1/2 cups)
HAZEL NUTS, coarsely chopped, toasted*	3-1/2 cups
CREAM, HEAVY	2 quarts

Procedure

1. Marinate candied fruit in maraschino liqueur.
2. Combine sugar and water; cook until syrup reaches soft ball stage (236°F.)
3. Pour syrup in fine stream into beaten egg whites, continuing to beat until mixture forms stiff peaks. Chill.
4. Add nuts to marinated fruits; fold into chilled meringue.
5. Whip cream. Fold into mixture, blending well.
6. Turn into 4-inch by 15-inch by 4-inch loaf pans. Freeze until firm.

Or almonds and pistachio nuts.

CHOCOLATE HIGH HATS

Yield: 40 portions (1/3 cup filling)

Ingredients

WHIPPED DESSERT MIX, CHOCOLATE FLAVOR	1 bag (15 ounces)
WATER, *ice-cold*	1 quart
FROZEN DESSERT SHELLS (page 100)	40
CHOCOLATE SAUCE	2-1/2 cups

Procedure

1. Combine dessert mix and water in mixer bowl. Blend thoroughly. Whip at high speed until light and fluffy, about 5 minutes.
2. Using a No. 12 scoop, fill frozen dessert shells with filling.
3. Freeze.
4. Just before serving, top each dessert with about 1 tablespoon of chocolate sauce.

FROZEN LEMON CUSTARD

Yield: 10 quarts

Ingredients

EGG WHITES	12 ounces (1-1/2 cups)
WATER	1 quart
INSTANT NONFAT DRY MILK	1 pound, 3 ounces
EGG YOLKS	8 ounces (1 cup)
SUGAR	2 pounds
LEMON PEEL, grated	1 tablespoon
LEMON JUICE	2 cups

Procedure

1. Put egg whites, water, and nonfat dry milk into mixer bowl. Beat at high speed until mixture is stiff, about 7 minutes.

2. Mix egg yolks, sugar, lemon peel, and juice with mixer at lowest speed. Fold in whipped milk mixture at lowest speed.

3. Pack into ten 1-quart ice cream cartons. Cover; store in freezer for 2 days, or until firm.

4. To serve, peel off carton and cut custard into slices.

Note

Freeze dessert in 6-ounce paper cups for individual portions, if desired.

Advisory Council for Jams, Jellies, and Preserves

Preserve-Topped a la Mode on Waffle

FROZEN LEMON DESSERT

Yield: 96 portions

Ingredients

GRAHAM CRACKER CRUMBS	2 pounds
SUGAR	3 cups
BUTTER, melted	3/4 pound
SUGAR	2-1/2 quarts
CORNSTARCH	1 cup
SALT	1 tablespoon
EGG YOLKS	48 (1 quart)
LEMON JUICE	1 quart
LEMON PEEL, grated	1/2 cup
EGG WHITES	48 (1-1/2 quarts)
CREAM, HEAVY	2 quarts
ALMONDS, slivered, toasted	1 quart

Procedure

1. Mix crumbs, first amount of sugar and melted butter. Press into three 12-inch by 20-inch by 2-1/2-inch pans lined with foil.

2. Mix sugar, cornstarch, and salt. Beat in egg yolks. Add lemon juice and peel. Cook in double boiler or steam jacket kettle until thickened, stirring constantly. Cool.

3. Beat egg whites until stiff but not dry. Gently fold into egg yolk mixture.

4. Whip cream; fold into mixture. Pour into crumb-lined pans; top with almonds.

5. Seal, label and freeze. When frozen, remove pans; stack packages.

LEMON-FILLED FROZEN DESSERT SHELLS

Yield: 40 portions

Ingredients

FROZEN DESSERT SHELLS (page 100)	40
LEMON PIE FILLING, CHILLED*	
OR LEMON PUDDING, CHILLED,	
OR LEMON ICE CREAM	
OR LEMON SHERBET	2-1/2 to 3 quarts

Procedure

Just before serving, fill each frozen shell with a No. 16 scoop of desired filling. Serve at once.

When using lemon pie filling, stir chilled filling until creamy.

Sunkist Growers, Inc.

Lemon Sherbet in Lemon Shells

FROZEN ANGEL FOOD PUDDING

Yield: 30 portions No. 51 souffle cups

Ingredients

GELATINE, UNFLAVORED	2 tablespoons
WATER, cold	1/4 cup
WATER, boiling	1 cup
SUGAR	1 cup
SALT	1/8 teaspoon
VANILLA	2 tablespoons
EGG WHITES	1 cup
WHIPPED CREAM, sweetened	1 quart

Procedure

1. Soften gelatine in cold water; dissolve in boiling water.
2. Add sugar and salt; stir until dissolved. Add vanilla.
3. Cool until slightly thickened.
4. Whip egg whites until stiff; fold into gelatine mixture.
5. Fold in the whipped cream; turn into No. 51 souffle cups. Freeze. Serve with a fudge sauce.

United Dairy Industry Association

Graham Cracker Crust Coats Triple Layer Bombe (Crust recipe, pp. 65–67)

REGAL CHOCOLATE MOUSSE

Yield: 2 gallons (64 1/2-cup portions)

Ingredients

CHOCOLATE, UNSWEETENED	1 pound
WATER	1-2/3 cups
SUGAR	1-3/4 pounds
SALT	3/4 teaspoon
EGG YOLKS, well beaten	10 ounces
VANILLA	2 tablespoons
CREAM, HEAVY	3 quarts

Procedure

1. Combine chocolate and water in saucepan. Cook over low heat, stirring vigorously, until blended. (Mixture will be very thick.)

2. Combine sugar and salt. Gradually stir into chocolate mixture. Continue to cook, stirring, until mixture is smooth and shiny and all sugar is dissolved, about 3 minutes.

3. Stir chocolate mixture slowly into beaten yolks. Cool until mixture is warm but not set (approximately 80° to 90°F.) Stir in vanilla.

4. Whip cream until thick and shiny but not stiff.

5. Gradually add chocolate mixture using low speed of mixer and just mixing until blended.

6. Chill in shallow pans or individual dessert dishes.

Note

For buffet service, pour into molds and freeze overnight. Unmold; garnish as desired.

FROZEN DESSERT SHELLS

Yield: 40 shells

Ingredients

WHIPPED TOPPING MIX	1 bag
NONFAT DRY MILK	1-1/3 cups
WATER, *ice-cold*	3-3/4 cups
SUGAR	2 tablespoons
VANILLA	1 tablespoon

Procedure

1. Combine all ingredients in 12-quart mixer bowl. Beat with wire whip at low speed for 30 seconds.
2. Scrape bottom and slides of bowl thoroughly.
3. Whip at high speed 5 to 8 minutes, or until soft peaks form.
4. Drop onto wax paper, using a No. 8 scoop (1/2 cup). Make indentation in each shell with back of scoop.
5. Freeze about 1 hour.

MOCHA WHIP

Yield: 28 1/2-cup portions

Ingredients

WHIPPED DESSERT MIX, CHOCOLATE	15 ounces
INSTANT COFFEE	1/4 cup
WATER, very cold	1 quart
WALNUTS, finely chopped	1 cup

Procedure

1. Combine dessert mix and coffee powder. Add water; beat according to label directions.
2. Fold in walnuts.
3. Ladle into shallow pans. Chill at least 2 hours. Or, freeze, allowing at least 4 hours.

PUDDINGS

MANY ADVANTAGES can be listed for puddings when the menu-maker's attention centers on desserts. In most instances, puddings are modest in cost, easy to make, and simple to serve. The American taste for them derives from English tradition, but many of today's recipes are strictly America's own.

Puddings embrace a wide variety of combinations ranging from the simple custard type to the rich, fruit-laden kind that requires long cooking in steam. Fruit crisps, cobblers, trifles, certain dumplings, and refrigerator cakes are all a part of the broad pudding classification.

As with fruit pies and fried desserts, many puddings are at their prime when freshly cooked and presented still warm. Some of the most delightful puddings are easy to make since part of the dessert can be prepared ahead. This advantage comes into play especially with puddings that rely on gelatines.

The simple, creamy puddings fashioned with cornstarch, tapioca, or rice are familiar to everyone. They have an unpretentious, homey quality that gives them a wide appeal. But perhaps the best aspect of these desserts is their almost unlimited capacity for change. They readily accept flavor variations and comely additions as well as all manner of dress-up touches that create irresistible eye appeal. Made on-premise or purchased ready-to-serve, puddings respond readily to the magic of new ideas.

Vanilla Cornstarch and Tapioca Puddings

VANILLA CORNSTARCH PUDDING lends itself to being served layered, marbled, or dished side-by-side with a complementary flavor in a sherbet or flat nappy dish. (To marble, place alternate spoonfuls of two different flavored puddings in a serving dish; insert a knife blade about an inch from the edge, and draw it in a circle through the puddings.)

SERVING SUGGESTIONS FOR VANILLA CORNSTARCH PUDDING

Layer parfait-fashion with:
Chocolate pudding
Butterscotch pudding

Marble with:
Chocolate pudding

Dish side-by-side with:
Chocolate pudding

For either type of vanilla pudding, cornstarch or tapioca, try the following serving suggestions.

SERVING TIPS

Flavor with:
Almond extract
Sherry
Brandy
Sherry with a hint of nutmeg

Fold in:
Chopped maraschino cherries
Coconut
Chopped nuts
Crushed pineapple, well-drained
Diced banana
Whipped cream or whipped topping

Layer with:
Sliced canned apricots
Sliced bananas and/or chocolate sauce

Amaretto di Saronno

Floating Island, Favorite from Victorian Times

Spiced blueberry sauce

Whole cranberry sauce

Flavored gelatine cubes

Macaroon crumbs

Marron pieces in syrup or Nesselrode sauce

Sliced peaches (sweetened fresh, or drained, frozen, or canned)

Cut-up prunes

Strawberry, raspberry, or apricot preserves

Sliced strawberries (sweetened, fresh, or just-thawed frozen)

Whipped topping and tart red jelly

Garnish with:

Whipped Cream, or Topping, and/or the following

Apricot halves or slices

Banana slices

Drizzles of butterscotch syrup

Chocolate curls

Chocolate sprinkles

Quarters of chocolate mint patties

Drizzles of chocolate syrup

Sprinkling of cinnamon

Maraschino cherries

Coconut (grated fresh; shredded, plain, toasted, tinted, or flaked)

Whole cranberry sauce

Slices or strips of dates

Flavored gelatine cubes

Strips of dried figs

Small bits of candied or preserved ginger

Jelly

Thin slices of kumquat (fresh or preserved)

Sprinkling of nutmeg

Chopped nuts

Orange (quarters of unpeeled slices; mandarin orange sections; small bits of candied peel; sprinkling of grated peel)

Peach slices

Crushed peanut brittle

Crushed peppermint candy

Halves of seeded prunes

Strawberries (whole, capped or uncapped; sliced)

For additional garnish suggestions see recipes for:

Cinnamon Nut Crumb Topping, page 268

No-Cook Plum Topping, page 274

Raspberry Whipped Cream, page 277

Red Raspberry Fruit Whip, page 273

Chocolate Pudding

SERVING SUGGESTIONS

Layer parfait-fashion with:
Vanilla pudding
Butterscotch pudding
Whipped topping

Dish side-by-side with:
Vanilla pudding in a sherbet dish or flat nappy dish

Marble with:
Vanilla pudding

Flavor with:
Almond extract
Sherry
Rum
Brandy

Fold in:
Diced banana
Coconut
Diced dates or figs
Miniature marshmallows
Chopped nuts
Crushed peanut brittle or peppermint candy

Garnish with:
Coffee-flavored whipped cream or topping
Amber whipped cream (see recipe, page 276)
Sour cream, plain or lightly sweetened
Whipped cream with orange marmalade folded in

Whipped cream or topping and/or:
  Roasted, diced almonds
  Banana or canned pear slices
  Chocolate curls
  Chocolate sprinkles
  Quarters of chocolate peppermint pattie
  Toasted coconut
  Cube of mint jelly
  Sprig of fresh mint
  Chopped nuts (peanuts, pecans, walnuts)
  Grated orange peel
  Slivers of candied orange peel
  Crushed peanut brittle or peppermint candy

Pacific Coast Canned Pear Service

Cubed Pears, New Note for Chocolate Pudding

Sauce with:

Vanilla custard sauce

Almond custard sauce

Mint-flavored marshmallow sauce, tinted a delicate pink or
green

Serve in:

Coffee, almond-flavored, or vanilla-flavored meringue shell

Frozen dessert shell

Dessert dish lined with lady fingers

Sherbet glass lined with vanilla wafers

Butterscotch Pudding

SERVING SUGGESTIONS

Layer parfait-fashion with:
Chocolate pudding
Vanilla pudding
Mincemeat sauce
Sliced bananas and/or crushed peanut brittle

Parfait Service for Butterscotch Pudding

Marble with:
Vanilla pudding
Chocolate pudding

Fold in:
Toasted coconut
Cut-up dates
Chopped nuts (almonds, filberts, peanuts, pecans, walnuts)
Puffed raisins

Garnish with:
Whipped cream or topping and/or the following
Roasted diced almonds
Drizzles of butterscotch or chocolate sauce
Chocolate sprinkles
Shredded coconut (plain or toasted)
Pecan halves
Chopped walnuts

Creamy
Rice Pudding

SERVING SUGGESTIONS

Flavor with:
Spices
Maple sugar or syrup
Grated lemon peel
Soluble coffee
   (Create a coffee variation by adding cut dates)

Fold in:
Raisins
Crushed pineapple, drained
Canned apricot slices, drained
Sliced peaches (canned or frozen), drained
   (Try garnishing the peach version with nutmeg-flavored
   whipped cream or topping)

Sauce with:
Cherry pie filling, thinned to sauce consistency
Brandied black cherry sauce
Chocolate sauce

Garnish with:
Whipped cream or topping and/or
A sprinkling of cinnamon
A dash of fresh ground nutmeg

DATE GRAHAM CRACKER ROLL

Yield: 384 portions

Ingredients

DATES, PITTED, CHOPPED	13-1/2 pounds
PECANS, chopped	5 pounds
MARSHMALLOWS, cut in quarters	20 pounds
GRAHAM CRACKER CRUMBS	20 pounds
CREAM, LIGHT	1-1/4 gallons
CREAM, HEAVY	8 quarts
SUGAR, CONFECTIONERS'	2 cups
VANILLA	2-2/3 tablespoons
MARASCHINO CHERRIES (optional)	as needed

Procedure

1. Combine dates, pecans, marshmallows, graham cracker crumbs, and light cream; mix well.

2. Shape into 32 rolls (approximately 2 pounds, 2 ounces each) making 2-1/2-inches in diameter. Wrap rolls in waxed paper; refrigerate overnight.

3. Whip cream with sugar and vanilla.

4. Cut each roll into 12 slices. Top with whipped cream. Garnish with maraschino cherry, if desired.

PINEAPPLE CHEESE DESSERT

Yield: 60 portions

Ingredients

GRAHAM CRACKER CRUMBS	1-1/2 pounds
SUGAR	5 ounces (3/4 cup)
BUTTER *OR* MARGARINE, softened	12 ounces
CRUSHED PINEAPPLE, CANNED, WITH SYRUP	1-3/4 quarts
GELATIN, ORANGE FLAVOR	1-1/2 pounds
WATER, hot	2-1/2 quarts
CREAM CHEESE, softened	2 pounds
ORANGE PEEL, grated	1 tablespoon
SUGAR	7 ounces (1 cup)
VANILLA	4 teaspoons
SOUR CREAM	2 quarts

Procedure

1. Mix crumbs, first amount of sugar, and butter. Press firmly into bottoms of three 13 inch by 9 inch pans.

2. Bake in oven at 350°F. 5 minutes. Cool.

3. Drain pineapple, reserving syrup.

4. Dissolve gelatin in hot water. Add syrup.

5. Add 1 quart of gelatin mixture to the drained pineapple. Set aside for a glaze.

6. Cool remainder of gelatin mixture.

7. Combine cheese, orange peel, remaining sugar, and vanilla; mix well. Gradually add cooled gelatin, blending well.

8. Fold in sour cream.

9. Pour into prepared crusts, allowing 2 quarts per pan. Chill until firm.

10. Top with pineapple mixture, allowing 2-1/2 cups per pan. Chill until glaze is firm.

ENGLISH TOFFEE DESSERT

Yield: 48 portions

Ingredients

VANILLA WAFERS, finely crushed	3 pounds (3 quarts)
NUT MEATS, finely chopped	1 pound (1 quart)
BUTTER, softened	3/4 pound
BUTTER	1-1/4 pounds
CONFECTIONERS' SUGAR, sifted	3 pounds
NONFAT DRY MILK	1/2 pound
EGG YOLKS	1-2/3 cups
CHOCOLATE, UNSWEETENED, melted	8 ounces
VANILLA	3 tablespoons
EGG WHITES	2-1/3 cups

Procedure

1. Mix crushed vanilla wafers and nut meats with softened butter. Use half of these crumbs to cover bottoms of two 9-inch by 15-inch by 2-inch pans.

2. Cream remaining butter. Add confectioners' sugar, nonfat dry milk, egg yolks, chocolate, and vanilla. Beat until smooth and fluffy.

3. Beat egg whites until stiff. Fold into chocolate mixture. Spread evenly over crumbs in pans. Cover with remaining crumbs.

4. Refrigerate for several hours. Cut in squares. Serve with whipped cream or topping.

DANISH APPLE PUDDING

Yield: 20 portions

Ingredients

CAKE CRUMBS	1-3/4 pounds
MARGARINE, melted	4 ounces
APPLE SAUCE	4 pounds
BROWN SUGAR	4 ounces
CINNAMON	1 teaspoon
CREAM, whipped	2 cups
COCONUT	4 ounces

Procedure

1. Mix crumbs with margarine; chill. Spread half of crumbs in bottom of 16-inch by 10-inch by 2-inch pan.

2. Mix apple sauce, sugar, and cinnamon. Spread half of apple sauce over crumbs; repeat layers.

3. Chill overnight.

4. Spread top with whipped cream; top with coconut.

The Rice Council

Banana Rice Custard

GINGER REFRIGERATOR PUDDING

Yield: 48 portions

Ingredients

GINGERSNAPS	2 pounds
BUTTER *OR* MARGARINE	12 ounces
CONFECTIONERS' SUGAR	2 pounds
EGGS	8
CREAM, HEAVY	3 cups
PINEAPPLE TIDBITS, drained	1 quart
BANANAS, sliced	8
WALNUTS, chopped	8 ounces

Procedure

1. Roll gingersnaps or put through the coarse screen of grinder to make crumbs.

2. Cream butter and sugar together. Add eggs; beat until fluffy.

3. Whip cream. Fold in pineapple, bananas, and nuts.

4. Butter a 12-inch by 18-inch by 2-inch pan. Cover bottom of pan with about 1/3 of the crumbs. Carefully spread sugar mixture over crumbs. Add another 1/3 of crumbs.

5. Spread fruit mixture carefully over second crumb layer. Sprinkle with remaining crumbs. Chill overnight. Cut into squares.

CHOCOLATE REFRIGERATOR CAKE

Yield: 24 portions

Ingredients

CHOCOLATE, SEMI-SWEET	1 pound
WATER	3 tablespoons
EGG YOLKS	8 (2/3 cup)
SUGAR, CONFECTIONERS'	4 tablespoons
WALNUT MEATS, chopped	1 cup
EGG WHITES	8 (1 cup)
HEAVY CREAM, whipped	
OR TOPPING, PREPARED	2 cups
LADY FINGERS, split	24

Procedure

1. Melt chocolate in top of double boiler over hot water. Add water; blend.

2. Remove from heat, add egg yolks one at a time, beating vigorously after each addition until smoothly blended.

3. Add sugar and walnuts; mix well.

4. Beat egg whites until stiff; fold gently into chocolate mixture along with whipped cream.

5. Line two 1-1/2-quart baking dishes or one 3-pound bread loaf pan with heavy waxed paper or foil, then line with lady fingers. Pour in the chocolate mixture.

6. Refrigerate 12 to 24 hours. Serve with additional whipped cream or topping, if desired.

GOLDEN RICE PUDDING

Yield: 63 1/2-cup portions

Ingredients

SUGAR	2-1/4 cups (1 pound)
SALT	3 tablespoons
GELATINE, unflavored	5 tablespoons
MILK	1 gallon
RICE, (EXTRA LONG GRAIN)	
cooked	4-1/2 quarts
VANILLA	4-1/2 teaspoons
CREAM, HEAVY	1 quart

Procedure

1. Mix sugar, salt, and gelatine in a saucepan; gradually stir in milk. Add rice.

2. Cover. Heat slowly, stirring occasionally until gelatine is dissolved, about 25 minutes.

3. Remove from heat; add vanilla. Cool to room temperature.

4. Whip cream; fold into rice mixture.

5. Turn into three 15-1/2-inch by 9-inch by 2-1/4-inch pans allowing 2-3/4 quarts per pan. Chill until firm.

6. Cut each pan into 21 portions. Serve with Red Raspberry Sauce or Cran-Orange Sauce, see following recipes.

RED RASPBERRY SAUCE

Yield: 3-1/4 quarts

Ingredients

RED RASPBERRIES, FROZEN,	
sweetened, thawed	10 pounds
CORNSTARCH	1 cup
WATER, cold	2-1/2 cups
LEMON JUICE	3/4 cup

Procedure

1. Sieve berries.

2. Blend cornstarch with water. Add to raspberry puree.

3. Cook, stirring constantly until thickened and clear. Add lemon juice. Chill.

CRAN-ORANGE SAUCE

Yield: 3-1/2 quarts

Ingredients

SUGAR	1/2 pound
CORNSTARCH	2/3 cup
SALT	2 teaspoons
ORANGE JUICE	6-1/2 cups
CRANBERRY JUICE	6-1/2 cups
BUTTER *OR* MARGARINE	3 tablespoons

Procedure

1. Mix sugar, cornstarch, and salt. Gradually stir in juices; mix well. Cook, stirring constantly until thickened and clear.

2. Add butter; stir until melted, chill.

Sliced Strawberry Sauce Brightens Rice Pudding

The Rice Council

PINEAPPLE RICE PUDDING WITH CARAMEL SAUCE

Yield: 20 3/4-cup portions, 1 ounce sauce

Ingredients

RICE PUDDING, READY-TO-SERVE	1 No. 10 can
PINEAPPLE TIDBITS, CANNED, drained	3 cups
MILK	1-1/3 cups
CORNSTARCH	1/4 cup
SALT	1/2 teaspoon
SUGAR, LIGHT BROWN	6 ounces
BUTTER *OR* MARGARINE	4 ounces
SUGAR, LIGHT BROWN	15 ounces

Procedure

1. Combine rice pudding and pineapple tidbits. Refrigerate several hours to blend flavors.

2. Mix milk with cornstarch, salt, and first amount of brown sugar in a heavy saucepan. Cook over medium heat, stirring often, until thick, clear, and smooth.

3. Add butter and remaining sugar; continue to cook, stirring constantly, until completely dissolved and mixture reaches boiling point. Serve warm or cool on portions of pudding.

MAPLE APPLES WITH RAISIN NUT DUMPLINGS

Yield: 48 portions (2 dumplings, 3/4 cup apples and syrup)

Ingredients

APPLE SLICES	2 No. 10 cans
BUTTER *OR* MARGARINE	1-1/2 pounds
APPLE JUICE	3 quarts
MAPLE BLENDED SYRUP	3 quarts
LEMON JUICE	3/4 cup
CINNAMON, GROUND	2 tablespoons
NUTMEG, GROUND	2 tablespoons
BISCUIT MIX	4 pounds
SUGAR, GRANULATED	1/2 cup
RAISINS	12 ounces (2-1/4 cups)
WALNUTS, coarsely chopped	2 cups
MILK	1-1/2 quarts

Procedure

1. Combine apple slices, butter, apple juice, maple syrup, lemon juice, and spices. Bring to a boil; simmer 5 minutes.

2. Combine biscuit mix, sugar, raisins, and walnuts.

3. Add milk, all at once, to dry ingredients. Mix until blended.

4. Divide hot apple mixture between two 12-inch by 20-inch by 2-inch baking pans. Using a No. 20 scoop, drop dumpling dough on top of hot apple mixture.

5. Bake, uncovered, in oven at 400°F. 10 to 15 minutes or until dumplings are lightly browned.

6. Serve warm.

Note

Apple mixture can be made in advance and refrigerated. Heat thoroughly before adding dumpling dough.

PLANTATION PARFAIT

Yield: 1-1/2 gallons pudding, approximately 1-1/2 quarts sauce,
48 portions

Ingredients

MILK, cold	5 quarts
PEANUT BUTTER, CREAMY	2 pounds, 13 ounces
INSTANT PUDDING, BUTTERSCOTCH	2 pounds, 8 ounces
CHOCOLATE CHIPS	1 pound, 12 ounces
BUTTER, MELTED	4 ounces
CONFECTIONERS' SUGAR, sifted	10 ounces
MILK	2-1/4 cups
VANILLA	1-3/4 teaspoons
WHIPPED CREAM *OR* TOPPING	3 cups
SALTED PEANUT HALVES	48
CHOCOLATE SPRINKLES	1/2 cup

Procedure

1. Pour milk into mixing bowl. Add peanut butter and pudding mix. Beat slowly until well mixed, about 1 minute. Let stand to thicken. Chill.

2. Melt chocolate chips in butter over hot water. Add sugar and milk gradually, blending well after each addition. Stir in vanilla. Chill thoroughly.

3. To serve, place alternate layers of chocolate sauce and peanut pudding in parfait dishes, ending with sauce. Garnish each portion with a tablespoon of whipped cream, a peanut half, and 1/2 teaspoon chocolate sprinkles.

Rice Pudding Layered with Cranberry Sauce, Parfait Style

HOT PEACH PUDDING

Yield: 24 portions

Ingredients

CLING PEACH SLICES	1 No. 10 can
LEMON JUICE	2 tablespoons
SUGAR, GRANULATED	1 cup
FLOUR, ALL-PURPOSE, sifted	2 ounces (1/2 cup)
SALT	1 teaspoon
CINNAMON	1 teaspoon
ROLLED OATS	1-1/2 cups
SUGAR, BROWN	10-1/2 ounces (1-1/2 cups, packed)
FLOUR, ALL-PURPOSE, sifted	6 ounces (1-1/2 cups)
SODA	1/2 teaspoon
BAKING POWDER	1/2 teaspoon
BUTTER *OR* MARGARINE	1/2 pound
ALMONDS, chopped	2 ounces (1/2 cup, scant)

Procedure

1. Drain peach slices thoroughly. Add lemon juice.

2. Combine sugar, first amount of flour, salt, and cinnamon. Add to peach slices; mix well. Turn into well oiled pudding pan, approximately 11 inches by 16 inches.

3. Mix rolled oats, brown sugar, remaining flour, soda, and baking powder. Cut in butter as for pie crust. Add almonds.

4. Spread oat mixture over peach mixture in pudding pan; pat down firmly.

5. Bake in oven at 350°F. for 45 minutes. Serve warm with cream or ice cream.

Note

Pudding may be prepared for baking ahead of time and refrigerated. Allow up to 30 minutes longer baking time if placed in oven at refrigerated temperature.

PEACH TRIFLE

Yield: 24 portions

Ingredients

VANILLA PUDDING AND PIE FILLING MIX	12 ounces (1/2 package)
MILK	1-1/2 quarts
ORANGE JUICE *OR* WHITE WINE	1-1/2 cups
ANGEL FOOD CAKE, 16 inches by 4-1/2 inches by 4 inches	2 loaves
STRAWBERRY JELLY	1-1/2 cups
CLING PEACH SLICES, drained	1-1/2 quarts
CREAM, WHIPPING	3 cups

Procedure

1. Prepare pudding according to package directions, using *only* 1-1/2 quarts of milk. Remove from heat; add 3/4 cup of the orange juice or wine. Cool.

2. Slice cake into lengthwise or crosswise slices 1/2 inch thick. Cut to fit bottom and sides of a 20-inch by 11-1/2-inch by 2-1/2-inch pan. Line pan with cake slices.

3. Drizzle remaining orange juice or wine over cake; spoon on jelly.

4. Arrange 1 quart of the peach slices over jelly layer.

5. Turn cooled pudding over peach slices; spread evenly.

6. Whip cream; spread over top. Garnish with remaining peach slices.

7. Refrigerate 3 to 4 hours. Cut into squares.

HA'PENNY PUDDING CAKE
(pictured opposite and on cover, upper inset)

Yield: Two 12-inch by 18-inch by 2-inch pans

Ingredients

CLING PEACH SLICES	2 No. 10 cans
APRICOTS, PITTED	1 No. 10 can
YELLOW SHEET CAKE, baked	1 sheet (18 inches by 26 inches by 1 inch)
PUDDING, READY-TO-SERVE, LEMON *OR* VANILLA	1 No. 10 can
WHIPPED TOPPING	as needed

Procedure

1. Drain peach slices.
2. Turn apricots into mixer bowl; whip to a coarse puree.
3. Divide cake in half, using one-half of the cake for each pan of pudding. Split each half of cake horizontally; place a layer in the bottom of each of two 12-inch by 18-inch by 2-inch pans.
4. Spoon apricot puree over cake allowing 2-1/4 cups per pan.
5. Spread a layer of pudding over puree, allowing 2-1/4 cups per pan.
6. Cover pudding with peach slices, allowing approximately 1-1/2 quarts per pan.
7. Place remaining cake on top of peaches. Spread with remaining apricot puree then remaining pudding. Arrange remaining peaches on top (repeating steps 4, 5 and 6).
8. Garnish top with whipped topping, using a pastry bag.

Ha'Penny Pudding Cake (Recipe, p. 126; color photo on cover, upper inset)

Spiced Topping Heightens Pudding Appeal

PEACH GELATIN SHORTCAKE A LA MODE

Yield: 24 portions

Ingredients

SLICED PEACHES, FROZEN OR CANNED	1-1/2 quarts
FRUIT JUICE AND HOT WATER, to equal	2 quarts
GELATIN, ORANGE *OR* RASPBERRY	12 ounces (1-3/4 cups)
SUGAR	1/4 cup
LEMON JUICE	1/4 cup
INDIVIDUAL SPONGE CAKE SHELLS	24
ICE CREAM, VANILLA	2-1/4 quarts

Procedure

1. Thaw peaches, if frozen. Drain peaches. Measure juice; add water to make required amount. Heat.

2. Dissolve gelatin and sugar in the hot liquid. Add lemon juice; cool at room temperature.

3. Place cake shells in pans 1/2 inch apart, or place in individual dishes. Pour half of the gelatin over cakes. Chill.

4. Add peaches to remaining gelatin. Chill until well thickened. (Should be consistency of a fruit glaze.) Spoon over sponge cake shells, covering tops and sides. Chill only until firm.

5. Serve topped with a No. 20 scoop of ice cream.

RICH SHORTCAKE BISCUITS

Yield: 85 2-1/4-inch biscuits

Ingredients

BISCUIT MIX	5 pounds
CREAM, 20%	2-1/2 pounds
WHIPPED CREAM *OR* TOPPING	to garnish

Procedure

1. Combine biscuit mix and cream; mix only enough to incorporate.
2. Knead lightly to smooth and shape dough.
3. Roll dough on floured cloth or bench. Cut with 2-1/4-inch cutter.
4. Bake according to package directions.
5. For shortcake: split baked biscuits; fill and cover with sweetened fruit.* Garnish with whipped cream or whipped topping, if desired.

*Fruits for shortcake:

Strawberries
Raspberries, red or black
Sliced peaches, fresh; frozen, thawed; or canned
Sliced apricots, canned
Sliced banana
Warm, cooked apple slices (poached in light syrup)
Warm fresh blueberry sauce
Strawberries and pineapple
Apricots and bananas

CAKES AND CHEESECAKES

TREMENDOUS SCOPE for customer-pleasing exists when cake is served. Nearly everyone, young and old, delights in the celebration of a special occasion with a festive, frosted cake. And there are few who don't enjoy cake in one of its many guises no matter what the day.

Plain or fancy, cake ranks among the leading dessert items. It holds its own among popular between-meal snacks, too. Beyond these familiar uses, cake can be baked in all possible shapes, flavors, and sizes to become the foundation for many different kinds of delectable dessert concoctions.

Today's cake mixes and ready-made baked items have sparked a lively challenge for the menu-maker. Their con-

Amaretto di Saronno

Liqueur-Flavored Cake: A Festive Conclusion

131

venience means a greater opportunity than ever before for imaginative combinations, new adaptations, and clever make-up tricks.

With a spirit of adventure and a little creative thought, you can transform cake into an almost limitless variety of wonderful desserts.

Pacific Coast Canned Pear Service

Spiced, Pear-Topped Sponge Cake Shell

Angel Food Cake

SUGGESTIONS FOR UNFROSTED
ANGEL FOOD CAKE

Serve portions of cake as an accompaniment to:
Fruit cups
Stewed or canned fruit
Apple sauce
Ice cream
Gelatin desserts

Top portions of cake with:
Ice cream and sauce
Sweetened fruit and whipped cream or whipped topping
A thickened fruit sauce such as prepared fruit pie filling
A spoonful of fluffy topping, such as fruit whip, flavored whipped cream, or flavored whipped topping
Fluffy topping with macaroon crumbs or crushed candy folded in
Cherry vanilla ice cream and a splash of Amaretto liqueur
Coffee ice cream, or coffee whipped cream, or whipped topping and chocolate sauce
Strawberry ice cream and sliced strawberry sauce
A mound of cocoa whipped cream and a garnish of crushed English toffee candy
Sweetened sliced peaches and whipped cream or whipped topping
Sliced bananas and caramel sauce with an "extra" of toasted slivered almonds
A spoonful of whipped cream or whipped topping and a sprinkling of chopped pistachio nuts

SUGGESTIONS FOR FROSTED
ANGEL FOOD CAKE

- Give the uncut cake a light coating of a thin glaze (lemon, orange, strawberry, chocolate, coffee, for example).
- Dress up the uncut cake by spreading it with a whipped-up butter cream frosting, then putting a border of sliced almonds around the top.
- Frost the uncut cake with a fluffy boiled frosting and decorate if desired (Plain, tinted, or toasted coconut; shaved chocolate; chocolate curls, and small dabs of fruit jam swirled into the frosting are all apt garnishes.)
- Spread top and sides of uncut cake with one of the flavor variations of whipped cream or whipped topping.
- Cover top and sides of uncut cake with swirls of whipped cream or whipped topping that has chopped maraschino cherries, nesselrode sauce, or cooled lemon pie filling folded into it.

United Dairy Industry Association

Black Forest Quickie: Chocolate Cake Layers and Cherry Ice Cream

FURTHER VARIATIONS

- *Layered Cake:* Cut round or loaf-shaped angel food cakes horizontally into three layers; reassemble spreading ice cream or a fluffy filling between the layers. Also spread filling over top and sides. (Whipped cream, whipped topping, or other fluffy mixtures work out well for spreading.)

- *Filled Cake:* Cut a one-inch slice off the top of the cake. Set aside. Hollow out a trench in the cake about two inches deep and two inches wide. Fill cavity with ice cream, a fruited Bavarian cream, or other appropriate mixture. Replace top. Spread over all with whipped cream or whipped topping. Chill or freeze according to the type of filling used.

United Dairy Industry Association

Toasted Angel Food Square with Sauced Ice Cream

Cake Layers

DRESSED-UP CAKE LAYERS are a marvelous way to extend the variety of cake desserts. Simple, unfrosted rounds of cake—made from a recipe, made from a mix, or purchased ready-baked—score new dessert laurels when topped and sauced, or split and filled, and cut into pie-shaped wedges.

ICE CREAM TOPPINGS

Cake and ice cream have been popular since "way back when." However, a cake blanketed with a layer of ice cream, then cut and sauced, is an exciting new variation of the a la mode style. There are dozens of delightful combinations easy to plan and to put into action. The following examples suggest a few.

With a white or yellow layer:

Ice Cream Flavor(s)	Sauce(s)
Vanilla	Pineapple, strawberry, or brandied black cherry
Pistachio	Peach
Strawberry	Pineapple
Coffee	Chocolate
Butter pecan	Butterscotch

With a chocolate layer:

Ice Cream Flavor(s)	Sauce(s)
Chocolate	Marshmallow or chocolate mint
Peppermint stick	Hot fudge
Vanilla	Caramel
Chocolate chip	Creme de cacao
Coffee	Date nut
Rum raisin	Caramel (with a dash of rum)

WHIPPED CREAM OR WHIPPED TOPPING

Spread a fluffy white covering of whipped cream or whipped topping over a cake layer in attractive swirls. The flavor is delicious by itself, and it gives excellent support to any decorative garnish or colorful sauce you may choose to add. Here are some combination ideas:

With a white or yellow layer:
Flaked coconut and bite-size pieces of peeled orange
Well-drained, canned peach slices with a red raspberry sauce

United Dairy Industry Association

Eye-Catching Cake Tops: Cake Layer with Ice Cream Layer on Top

With a white, yellow, or chocolate layer:
Sliced ripe banana and coarsely chopped walnuts
Crushed almond brittle and butterscotch sauce
A broad band of chocolate or apricot sauce across the
portions

FLAVORED WHIPPED CREAM
OR WHIPPED TOPPING

*Change the flavor of the whipped cream or whipped topping
to add new originality and sparkle to the cake layer theme.
Garnishes, as always, give an extra touch. (See Index for list-
ings of topping and sauce recipes.)*

With a white or yellow layer:
Raspberry or strawberry whipped cream or whipped topping with a garnish or sauce of matching fruit
Prune whipped cream or whipped topping with pieces of
cooked prune folded in and a garnish of chopped nuts
Lemon whipped cream or whipped topping with cold lemon
pie filling folded in, garnished with soft cake crumbs

With a chocolate layer:
Coffee whipped cream or whipped topping, and a band of
chocolate sauce across the portions

With a white, yellow, or chocolate layer:
Amber whipped cream or whipped topping garnished with
strips of fresh dates or chopped roasted almonds
Cocoa whipped cream garnished with chopped nuts, shaved
chocolate, or drizzles of chocolate glaze

SOUR CREAM TOPPING

Sour cream used as a topping has its own special charm. Simply dress it up with a little sugar and a touch of vanilla. Add a small amount of dissolved gelatine, if desired, to give added stiffening.

With a white or yellow layer:
Strawberry sauce and a fresh strawberry garnish
Sliced peaches with peach sauce
Apricot sauce

With a chocolate layer:
Garnish of almond crunch or chocolate curls
A wide band of chocolate sauce across each wedge

Frozen Food Opportunity Time/Institutions Magazine

Easy Elegance for Cake Layers

FILLINGS

Another array of taste-tempting desserts can be created by splitting a cake layer horizontally, introducing a filling, replacing the top, then giving the cake an attractive finish.

Fillings include pastry cream, prepared pudding and pie fillings, and puddings that come ready-to-serve. These can be varied by adding flavoring, combining with fruits, or folding in nuts. In addition there are numerous jellies and preserves. Suggestions for finishing the top include confectioners' sugar, various glazes, and whipped cream or whipped topping with one of the many possible flavor changes.

Here are a few combinations to try with white or yellow cake—use these and expand with your own ideas when you serve chocolate cake.

Filling(s)	Topping(s)
Tart red jelly	Confectioners' sugar
Pastry cream flavored with rum or almond	Chocolate glaze
Vanilla pudding flavored with rum or almond	Whipped cream or topping with a hint of nutmeg
Vanilla pudding flavored with almond and a layer of sliced peaches	Confectioners' sugar
Vanilla pudding spread with nesselrode sauce	Whipped cream or topping with maraschino cherry garnish
Lemon pudding or pie filling	Thin fresh lemon glaze
Lightly sweetened ricotta cheese with cut dates and vanilla flavoring	Confectioners' sugar
Vanilla pudding and a layer of sliced bananas	Chocolate glaze
Butterscotch pudding with chopped pecans	Amber whipped cream or topping
Pineapple, peach, or berry pie filling	Whipped cream or topping, or confectioners' sugar
Vanilla pudding spread with apricot preserves	Coffee glaze

SPOOK CAKES

Yield: 48 portions

Ingredients

CHOCOLATE FROSTED CUPCAKES	48
VANILLA ICE CREAM	1 gallon
SEMI-SWEET CHOCOLATE PIECES	1/3 cup
MARASCHINO CHERRIES, cut in	
8 strips each	6

Procedure

1. Cut cone-shaped pieces out of tops of cupcakes.
2. Place a No. 12 scoop of ice cream on cupcake. Top with cone-shaped pieces of cake placed upside down at an angle.
3. To make face, arrange 3 chocolate pieces on ice cream for eyes and nose, and a sliver of cherry for mouth.

MERINGUE LAYERS (FOR SCHAUM TORTE)

Yield: 12 8-inch rounds

Ingredients

EGG WHITES	2-1/4 cups
VANILLA	2 tablespoons
CREAM OF TARTAR	1-1/2 teaspoons
SALT	3/4 teaspoon
SUGAR	1-3/4 pounds
ALMONDS, slivered	1 cup

Procedure

1. Combine egg whites, vanilla, cream of tartar, and salt; beat until foamy.
2. Gradually add sugar, continuing to beat until very stiff.
3. Spread meringue onto paper-covered baking sheets to form 12 8-inch rounds. Sprinkle with almonds.
4. Bake in oven at 275°F. for 1 hour. Turn off heat; let remain in oven at least another hour.
5. Cool; lift meringues from paper. For torte: Arrange layers, spreading lemon filling, whipped cream and strawberries, or other desired filling between the rounds.

MEXICAN ALMOND CAKE

Yield: 4 cakes

Ingredients

ALMONDS, WHOLE, BLANCHED	1/4 cup
WATER	1/3 cup
GREEN FOOD COLORING	1 teaspoon
ALMONDS, WHOLE, BLANCHED	1/4 cup
WATER	1/3 cup
RED OR ORANGE FOOD COLORING	1 teaspoon
ALMONDS, WHOLE, BLANCHED	1 quart
SUGAR	4 pounds, 6 ounces
WATER	1 quart
MUSCATEL WINE*	2-2/3 cups
POUND CAKE, cut into 1-inch cubes	3 pounds (1-3/4 gallons)
EGG YOLKS, beaten	20 (1-2/3 cups)
ALMOND EXTRACT	4 teaspoons
SALT	2 teaspoons

continued next page

MEXICAN ALMOND CAKE, *cont'd.*

Procedure

1. Combine first amount of almonds and water; color with green food coloring.

2. Combine next amount of almonds and water; color with red or orange food coloring.

3. Let almonds stand several hours or overnight until highly collored; drain.

4. Grind remaining almonds in electric blender or food chopper.

5. Combine sugar and remaining water in a saucepan. Bring to a boil; simmer 15 minutes.

6. Pour half (about 4-1/2 cups) of syrup into a bowl; cool. Add wine and cake cubes; toss lightly to soak cake.

7. Add ground almonds to remaining syrup in pan. Mix in egg yolks, a small amount at a time. Cook, stirring, over medium heat until thickened. Add almond extract and salt.

8. Generously butter four 1-1/4- or 1-1/2-quart ring molds.

9. Place 1 cup of prepared cake cubes in each mold. Top with 2/3 cup of ground almond mixture. Repeat layers making 3 layers of cake and 3 of almond mixture in each mold.

10. Bake in oven at 325°F. about 55 minutes or until top is lightly browned and dry to touch.

11. Cool in mold for 30 minutes. Loosen sides with knife or spatula; turn out into serving plates. Cover; let stand several hours or overnight (cakes keep well several days.)

12. Garnish with colored almonds.

Or other sweet dessert wine.

DANUBE TORTE

Yield: 8 cakes

Ingredients

SEMI-SWEET CHOCOLATE	3 pounds
BUTTER *OR* MARGARINE	2 pounds
WATER	2 cups
EGG YOLKS, slightly beaten	1 pound, 10 ounces
CONFECTIONERS' SUGAR	4-1/2 ounces
VANILLA	3 tablespoons
FILBERTS, coarsely ground, toasted	1 pound, 10 ounces
LOAF POUND CAKES, baked, cooled	8 cakes (12 ounce or 1 pound size)
FILBERTS, SLICED	as needed

Procedure

1. Heat chocolate, butter, and water in heavy pan over low heat until blended, stirring often.

2. Cool. Stir in egg yolks, sugar, and vanilla.

3. Chill mixture about 30 to 45 minutes or until of spreading consistency.

4. Split cakes horizontally into 6 layers each. Spread chocolate mixture over all but the 8 top layers. Sprinkle chocolate frosted layers with ground filberts.

5. Stack layers, re-forming the 8 cakes, place unfrosted layers on top.

6. Frost top and sides. Garnish with sliced filberts. Chill thoroughly.

DOBOS TORTE

Yield: One 8-inch torte

Ingredients

BUTTER SPONGE CAKE LAYERS, 8-INCH	4
BUTTER *OR* MARGARINE	3/4 pound
SUGAR, CONFECTIONERS', sifted	2 cups
EGG YOLKS, unbeaten	3
SEMI-SWEET CHOCOLATE PIECES	12 ounces
SUGAR, GRANULATED	2/3 cup
WATER	1/3 cup
CREAM OF TARTAR	1/4 teaspoon
FILBERTS *OR* ALMONDS, toasted chopped	1 cup

Procedure

1. Cut layers in two horizontally to make 8 layers in all.

2. Cream butter until fluffy; add confectioners' sugar gradually, continuing to beat. Add egg yolks, one at a time, beating until very fluffy.

3. Melt chocolate over hot water. Cool. Blend cooled chocolate into butter mixture.

4. Reserve one split layer of cake. Put remaining layers together with frosting between, allowing about 2/3 cup frosting per layer.

5. Combine granulated sugar, water, and cream of tartar. Bring mixture to a boil, stirring. Cook until just golden. Remove from heat; stir until bubbles disappear.

6. Pour over top of reserved layer. Spread quickly.

7. Before caramel hardens, score to mark off portions, using a well-buttered knife. Place glazed layer on top of torte.

8. Spread remaining icing around sides of torte. Cover sides with chopped nuts.

SICILIAN RICOTTA CAKE

Yield: Two 9-inch cakes

Ingredients

CHOPPED NATURAL ALMONDS	9 ounces (2 cups)
RICOTTA CHEESE	1 quart
MIXED CANDIED FRUITS, diced	10 ounces (1-1/3 cups)
SUGAR	5 ounces (2/3 cup)
SWEET CHOCOLATE, grated	4 ounces
ALMOND EXTRACT	2 teaspoons
LEMON PEEL, grated	2 teaspoons
SPONGE CAKE, 9-inch round layers, 3/4-inch thick	6 layers
RASPBERRY OR APRICOT JAM	10 ounces (1 cup)
SWEETENED WHIPPED CREAM *OR* TOPPING	1 quart
CHOPPED NATURAL ALMONDS	4-1/2 ounces (1 cup)
BUTTERCREAM ROSES	16 or 20
ANGELICA *OR* GREEN CANDIED FRUIT	as needed

Procedure

1. Combine first amount of almonds, ricotta cheese, fruit, sugar, chocolate, almond extract, and lemon peel; mix.

2. For each cake, use 3 sponge cake layers. Start with cake on bottom; spread with 15 ounces (about 1-1/2 cups) cheese mixture.

3. Place second layer on top; spread with 15 ounces cheese mixture. Spread with 5 ounces (1/2 cup) of the jam. Place third layer on top.

4. Cover top and sides of cake with whipped cream, allowing 2 cups per cake. Make a border of remaining chopped almonds around base, allowing 1/2 cup per cake.

5. Score top of cake to mark 8 or 10 portions. Make a border of the buttercream roses, placing one on each wedge. Add 2 small pieces of angelica to each rose to represent leaves.

ANGEL FOOD WITH CHERRY
MACAROON TOPPING

Yield: 24 portions

Ingredients

CREAM, HEAVY	1 quart
MACAROONS, crumbled	24
MARASCHINO CHERRIES, chopped, drained	1 cup
ALMONDS, chopped	1 cup
ANGEL FOOD CAKES, 10-INCH, UNICED	2

Procedure

1. Whip cream. Fold in macaroons, cherries, and almonds. Chill thoroughly.

2. Cut cakes into wedges. Serve with topping.

California Foods Research Institute

Gateau Sans-Souci

VIENNESE LAYER CAKE

Yield: One 9-inch cake

Ingredients

DEVIL'S FOOD LAYERS, 9-INCH	2
MOCHA CREAM ICING (*see recipe, opposite*)	as needed
CHOCOLATE SPRILLS OR SHOT	1/4 cup
WALNUTS, chopped	1 cup
CHOCOLATE WAFER WEDGES*	12

Procedure

1. Split devil's food layers into two layers each.
2. Assemble a 4-layer cake, spreading mocha icing between each layer and on top and sides.
3. Score or mark top of cake into serving pieces. Using a small star tube, swirl a decoration on each marked-off portion from center to near outer edge, ending in a small rosette. Scallop an edging of icing around top of cake. Pipe a rosette of icing in center of cake.
4. Sprinkle rosettes carefully with chocolate sprills. Cover sides of cake with chopped walnuts.
5. Stand a chocolate wafer wedge against each swirl of icing on top of cake.

To make chocolate wafer wedges: melt semi-sweet chocolate at 90°F. Spread a thin layer on a sheet of parchment paper. Let cool at a temperature of 50°F. When set, mark off in 2-inch by 3-inch rectangles. Cut each rectangle into two wedges by cutting diagonally, corner to corner.

MOCHA CREAM ICING
(for Viennese Layer Cake)

Yield: 12 pounds

Ingredients

SHORTENING, EMULSIFIER TYPE	2-1/2 pounds
SHORTENING, ALL-PURPOSE, POURABLE	1 pound (2 cups)
SALT	1 tablespoon
NONFAT DRY MILK SOLIDS	1/2 pound
INSTANT COFFEE	4 teaspoons
SUGAR, CONFECTIONERS'	5 pounds
WATER, lukewarm (110°F.)	2 cups
CORN SYRUP	1/3 cup
CHOCOLATE, UNSWEETENED, melted	1-1/2 pounds
VANILLA	as needed

Procedure

1. Place shortenings, salt, nonfat dry milk, coffee, confectioners' sugar, water, and corn syrup in mixing bowl. Use paddle beater. Mix at medium speed until well blended.

2. Add melted chocolate, continuing to mix at medium speed until desired lightness is obtained, (about 10 minutes). Add vanilla, as desired.

GELATIN GLAZED UPSIDE DOWN CAKE

Yield: Eight 9-inch cakes

Ingredients

GELATIN, STRAWBERRY FLAVOR	1-1/2 pounds
WATER, boiling	2 quarts
FROZEN STRAWBERRY HALVES (WITH JUICE), thawed	2 quarts (5 pounds)
CAKE LAYERS, 9-INCH (WHITE OR YELLOW)	8

Procedure

1. Dissolve gelatin in boiling water. Cool.

2. Add thawed strawberries with juice. Chill until slightly thickened.

3. Allow 2 cups gelatin mixture for each cake layer. Put about 1-1/3 cups in a 9-inch layer pan. Place cake layer on gelatin, top side up. Spoon remaining gelatin mixture around sides of cake. Chill until firm.

4. Unmold. Garnish portions with whipped cream or prepared whipped topping, whole berries and mint, if desired.

Amaretto di Saronno

Checker Board Cake (Recipe p. 154)

CHOCOLATE ALMOND LAYER CAKE

Yield: Two 9-inch cakes

Ingredients

CHOCOLATE, UNSWEETENED	6 ounces
BUTTER *OR* MARGARINE	8 ounces
SHORTENING	5-1/4 ounces
	(3/4 cup)
EGG YOLKS	4
ALMOND EXTRACT	3/4 teaspoon
RED FOOD COLORING (optional)	1/4 teaspoon
CONFECTIONERS' SUGAR, sifted	9 to 10 ounces
	(2 to 2-1/4 cups)
CAKE LAYERS, YELLOW, 9-INCH	4
ALMOND SPLITS, blanched	1/2 cup

Procedure

1. Melt chocolate over hot water or very low heat. Cool slightly.

2. Cream butter and shortening together at medium speed of mixer until blended.

3. Blend in chocolate, egg yolks, almond extract, and food coloring.

4. Turn mixer to low speed. Gradually add sugar to desired spreading consistency.

5. Spread frosting between layers and on top and sides of cakes. Stand almond splits in icing, arranging in 3 circles to form a border around top of each cake.

BOSTON CREAM PIE
WITH MINCEMEAT FILLING

Yield: Eight 9-inch layers

Ingredients

BUTTERSCOTCH PUDDING *OR*	
PIE FILLING, cooked	2-1/4 quarts
RUM EXTRACT	1 teaspoon
MINCEMEAT, PREPARED	3 cups
CAKE LAYERS, 9-INCH, split	
(WHITE CAKE, WHOLE EGG	
CAKE, *OR* SPONGE CAKE)	8
CONFECTIONERS' SUGAR	as needed

Procedure

1. Let cooked butterscotch pudding cool slightly; add rum extract and mincemeat. Cover closely with paper; chill.
2. Stir chilled pudding until smooth and glossy.
3. Fill split cake layers allowing 1-1/2 cups filling per layer.
4. Sprinkle tops with confectioners' sugar.

ORANGE-RUM CHIFFON CAKE

Yield: 24 portions

Ingredients

RUM	2/3 cup
ORANGE JUICE, UNSWEETENED	2/3 cup
SUGAR, GRANULATED	1 cup
ORANGE PEEL, grated	1 teaspoon
ORANGE CHIFFON CAKE	2 8-inch cakes

Procedure

1. Combine rum, orange juice, sugar, and orange peel in a small saucepan; bring to a boil. Lower heat; simmer 10 minutes. Cool.
2. Spoon orange syrup evenly over cakes, allowing it to soak into cake gradually. Refrigerate 2 hours before serving.
3. Cut cakes into 12 portions each.

FANDANGO CAKE

Yield: 24 portions

Ingredients

ANGEL FOOD CAKE, 10-INCH ROUND	2 cakes
CREAM, HEAVY	1 quart
SUGAR	1/2 cup
VANILLA	2 teaspoons
SALT	1/8 teaspoon
RASPBERRY SHERBET	1/2 quart
FRUIT COCKTAIL, drained	1 quart
LEMON SHERBET	1/2 quart
WHIPPED CREAM, sweetened	as needed

Procedure

1. Slice each cake into three horizontal layers.
2. Whip cream with sugar, vanilla, and salt.
3. Combine raspberry sherbet with 1-1/2 cups fruit cocktail.
4. Combine lemon sherbet with 1-1/2 cups fruit cocktail.
5. Working quickly, spread half of raspberry sherbet mixture on bottom layer of each cake. Cover with center layers.
6. Top center layers with lemon sherbet mixture. Cover with remaining layers.
7. Spread tops and sides of each cake with sweetened whipped cream. Garnish tops of cakes with remaining fruit cocktail. Freeze.

CHECKERBOARD CAKE
(see picture, p. 150)

Yield: 1 cake

Ingredients

POUND CAKE, FROZEN, thawed	1 12-ounce loaf
POUND CAKE, CHOCOLATE, FROZEN, thawed	1 12-ounce loaf
CHOCOLATE, UNSWEETENED, melted	1 ounce
INSTANT COFFEE POWDER	2 tablespoons
AMARETTO LIQUEUR	1/2 cup
BUTTER *OR* MARGARINE, softened	4 ounces
SUGAR, CONFECTIONERS'	1 pound
ORANGE PEEL, slivered, from	1 orange
AMARETTO LIQUEUR	1/3 cup

Procedure

1. Trim crusts from cakes.
2. Cut each cake lengthwise into three strips. Cut each strip lengthwise into halves making 6 plain strips and 6 chocolate strips.
3. Combine melted chocolate, instant coffee powder, first amount of liqueur, butter, and sugar. Beat until smooth and fluffy.
4. Combine orange peel and remaining liqueur; cook until peel is glazed. Cool.
5. Place one chocolate strip on a serving platter or tray; spread one side of strip with frosting. Press one plain strip in frosting. Repeat to make a layer of 4 strips.
6. Spread top with frosting.
7. Form the second layer over the first, starting with a plain strip. Proceed as before, ending with a chocolate strip.
8. Spread top of second layer with frosting.
9. Form the third layer, starting with a chocolate strip, ending with a plain strip.
10. Frost top and sides of cake. Deocrate with remaining frosting, using pastry bag with a star tip.
11. Garnish with glazed orange peel. Chill until ready to serve.

COCONUT-CINNAMON LOGS

Yield: 48

Ingredients

SUGAR	1 cup
RED CINNAMON CANDIES	1 cup
WATER	1-1/3 cups
ANGEL FOOD CAKES, 12-OUNCE LOAVES	2
COCONUT, FLAKED *OR* SHREDDED (firmly packed)	3 cups

Procedure

1. Combine sugar, cinnamon candies, and water in a small sauce pan.
2. Boil, stirring frequently, until candies dissolve and syrup begins to thicken or reaches 220°F.
3. Slice cake into 1-inch slices. Cut each slice into three "fingers".
4. Pour cinnamon syrup into a measure.
5. Pick up each piece of cake with tongs; quickly dip into syrup.
6. Place dipped cake pieces on a wire rack to drip.
7. Roll in coconut. Cool before serving.

APRICOT RIPPLED CAKE

Yield: 20 portions

Ingredients

APRICOTS, DRIED	3 cups (14 ounces)
ANGEL FOOD CAKE	2 8-inch cakes

Procedure

1. Wash apricots. Place in a 1-quart saucepan. Cover with water; simmer, uncovered, 30 minutes or until fruit is tender.
2. Drain apricots; sieve.
3. Cut cake in 10 equal-sized sections, cutting down to within 1/2 inch of bottom of cake.
4. Spread cut surfaces of cake with sieved apricots, using a spatula.
5. To serve; cut cake mid-way between apricot-filled spaces.

FILLED ANGEL FOOD CAKE

Yield: One 10-inch cake

Ingredients

ANGEL FOOD CAKE, 10-INCH ROUND	1 cake
MARSHMALLOWS, MINIATURE	1/2 pound
SALT	1/4 teaspoon
WATER	1/3 cup
SEMI-SWEET CHOCOLATE PIECES	1 cup (6 ounces)
CREAM, HEAVY	1 cup
ALMOND EXTRACT	1/8 teaspoon

Procedure

1. Cut a 1-inch slice across top of cake. Lift off; set aside.
2. Hollow out a trench in cake 2 inches wide and 2 inches deep.
3. Tear hollowed-out pieces of cake into small cubes; reserve.
4. Combine marshmallows, salt, and water. Heat over moderate heat until marshmallows are melted, stirring constantly. Remove from heat; add chocolate pieces. Stir until almost melted. Cool.
5. Whip cream; add almond extract. Fold into the cooled chocolate mixture.
6. Spread half of chocolate mixture into cake trench. Press cake cubes on top.
7. Spread with remaining chocolate mixture. Cover with cake top. Chill 3 to 4 hours or freeze.
8. Serve with chocolate sauce, or whipped cream, as desired.

LEMON ANGEL CAKE

Yield: Two 10-inch tube pans, 16 to 20 portions each

Ingredients

GELATINE, UNFLAVORED	2 tablespoons
SUGAR	1 cup
SALT	1/4 teaspoon
EGGS, beaten	4
WATER	1 cup
FROZEN LEMONADE- CONCENTRATE	2 6-ounce cans
EVAPORATED MILK, thoroughly chilled	2 14-1/2-ounce cans
ANGEL FOOD CAKE, 10-INCH SIZE	2

Procedure

1. Mix gelatine, sugar, and salt.
2. Add eggs and water; heat, stirring, until gelatine dissolves.
3. Remove from heat; stir in the lemonade concentrate.
4. Chill until mixture begins to thicken.
5. Whip the thoroughly chilled evaporated milk to consistency of whipped cream.
6. Fold whipped milk into partially thickened lemon mixture.
7. Rub brown crumbs off the cakes. Tear cakes into bite-size pieces.
8. Cover bottom of two 10-inch tube pans with layer of gelatine mixture.
9. Arrange 1/4 of cake on layer of gelatine in each pan. Add another layer of lemon mixture. Repeat, making two layers of cake and three of gelatine. Chill until firm. Unmold and serve.

Note

Left-over white or angel food cake may be used.

CHERRY ANGEL CAKE DESSERT

Yield: 48 portions

Ingredients

WATER, boiling	2 quarts
MARASCHINO CHERRY JUICE	2 cups
GELATIN, CHERRY FLAVOR	24 ounces
FROZEN SLICED PEACHES	2-1/2 pounds
SALT	1/2 teaspoon
LEMON JUICE	1 tablespoon
VANILLA ICE CREAM	2 quarts
MARASCHINO CHERRIES, drained, chopped	2 cups
ANGEL FOOD CAKES, 9-INCH	4
WHIPPED CREAM *OR* TOPPING, for garnish	as needed
MARASCHINO CHERRIES, WHOLE	48

Procedure

1. Combine boiling water and maraschino cherry juice. Add cherry gelatin; stir to dissolve.

2. Chop frozen peaches coarsely; add to the gelatin mixture, breaking apart as they thaw. Add salt and lemon juice.

3. Add ice cream in large chunks; stir, blending into mixture as it melts. Add chopped cherries.

4. Divide mixture between four 4-quart mixing bowls. (Mixture will thicken fast). As it thickens, push a whole angel food cake, upside down, in the middle of each bowl of gelatin mixture.

5. Place a plate over the cakes; put a light weight on the plate to hold it down until the gelatin stiffens. (Do not use a heavy weight. It will crush the cake and make it heavy). Chill.

6. Remove weight when gelatin sets, about 15 minutes.

7. To unmold, dip bowls in warm water; run spatula around edge; shake loose and invert onto sheet pans.

8. Cut dessert into wedges. Garnish portions with whipped cream or topping and whole cherry.

SUNRISE CAKE

Yield: 24 portions (1-1/2 quarts sauce)

Ingredients

CANNED CLING PEACH HALVES	
(24 TO 30 COUNT)	1 No. 10 can
SYRUP FROM PEACHES	4-1/2 cups
SUGAR, BROWN (PACKED)	3/4 cup
CORNSTARCH	1/3 cup
BUTTER *OR* MARGARINE	1/4 pound
RUM LIGHT,	1/3 cup
OR RUM EXTRACT	1 teaspoon
LOAF ANGEL FOOD (16 inches	
by 4-1/2 inches by 4 inches)	2 loaves
BUTTER *OR* MARGARINE, melted	as needed
STRAWBERRY JELLY	1/2 cup
COCONUT, SHREDDED, toasted	as needed

Procedure

1. Drain peach halves, reserving required amount of syrup.

2. Combine syrup, sugar, and cornstarch. Cook until thickened. Remove from heat; blend in butter and rum. Keep warm.

3. Cut each cake into 12 thick slices. Brush cake slices with melted butter. Place on bun pans; toast under broiler until golden brown.

4. To serve: arrange peach half, cup side up, on toasted cake slice. Place a teaspoon of strawberry jelly in cavity of peach. Ladle 2 ounces warm sauce over cake and fruit. Sprinkle with coconut.

LOVE CAKE SARONNO
(pictured on cover, main image)

Yield: Two 9-inch cakes

Ingredients

ANGEL FOOD CAKES, 9-INCH	2
AMARETTO LIQUEUR	3/4 cup
ICE CREAM, PISTACHIO, slightly softened	1 quart
ICE CREAM, STRAWBERRY, slightly softened	1 quart
CREAM, HEAVY*	1 quart
AMARETTO LIQUEUR	1/4 cup
CHOCOLATE MORSELS, SEMISWEET	12 ounces

Procedure

1. Cut each cake into three layers, using a sharp, serrated knife. Sprinkle layers with first amount of liqueur.

2. Place bottom layer of each cake on a serving plate or tray. Working quickly, spread with pistachio ice cream. Cover each with a second layer of cake; spread with strawberry ice cream. Top with remaining cake layers.

3. Place in freezer.

4. Combine cream and remaining liqueur; beat until thick and shiny. Spread sides and top of cakes; return to freezer.

5. Melt chocolate over very low heat until smooth. Spread in a layer 1/4-inch thick on foil. Chill until chocolate hardens. With a small heart-shaped cutter, cut hearts out of chocolate. Arrange in a border around top and base of cakes. Return cakes to freezer.

If desired, use 2 quarts prepared whipped topping in place of cream; fold in second amount of liqueur.

Cheesecake

TOPPINGS

Raisin Poppyseed Cheesecake Topping, see recipe page 169.

Coconut-Pecan Topping, see recipe page 265

Sour cream, plain, or lightly sweetened, and flavored with grated orange peel

Sour cream and a sprinkling of brown sugar (pressed through a sieve)

FRUIT GLAZES

Apricot

Berry (Blueberry, Boysenberry, Raspberry, Strawberry)

Blueberry with orange sections

Bing cherry

Bing cherry and sliced peach

Red cherry

Fresh orange

Peach

Pineapple

Pineapple and apricot

Pineapple and strawberry

OTHER GLAZES

Thinned orange marmalade or apricot preserves

Melted jelly

Chocolate glaze, spread in a thin layer or drizzled in a lacy pattern

Maple or caramel syrup

GARNISHES

Before garnishing, brush top of cake with syrup or spread with whipped cream, whipped topping, or sour cream, to help make sure that garnishes will adhere to cake. Most garnishes are effective when arranged as a border.

Crunch:
Cereal crunch
Almond crunch
Crushed peanut or almond brittle
Spiced graham cracker crumbs

Nuts:
Chopped pistachio nuts
Roasted, chopped almonds
Pecan or walnut halves, plain or glazed
Whole blanched almonds, with the rounded ends coated with chocolate
Chopped filberts
Toasted coconut
Split halves of blanched almonds—try four pieces arranged in a flower shape to decorate each portion of cake

Fruit:
Strawberries
Small clusters of sugared grapes
Half slices of unpeeled orange
Banana slices, cut diagonally
Mandarin orange sections
Thinly sliced kumquats (fresh or preserved)
Maraschino cherries—try halves with a mint leaf or two
Halves or quarters of sliced pineapple
Strips of fresh dates
Halves of seeded grapes, arranged in clusters or in clover leaf shape

Miscellaneous:

Miniature rolled cookies

Slivers of candied orange peel

A liberal sprinkling of confectioners' sugar

FURTHER SUGGESTIONS

- Coat with maple or caramel syrup and add sprinkling of toasted sesame seeds.
- Spread whipped cream or whipped topping over cake, or spoon on in mounds to form border. Decorate with shaved chocolate, chocolate curls, or grated orange peel.
- Border with whipped topping; close inside, add second but narrower band of chopped nuts.
- Pipe on whipped cream or topping, lattice-fashion, over top of either plain cheesecake or cake with bright fruit glaze.
- Spread whipped cream, whipped topping, or sour cream over top of cake, together with bands of crumb mixture. Arrange either lattice-fashion or in series of concentric circles. (See Index for recipes for Cinnamon Nut Crumb Topping, Cereal Crunch Topping, and Almond Crunch.)

Amaretto di Saronno

Gala Garnish for Cheesecake: Coffee-Flavored Whipped Cream Rosettes

- Spread sour cream on top of cake; add raspberry jam to create "zebra" pattern. To make pattern, pipe narrow lines of jam across the cream-topped cake, spacing rows evenly and keeping them parallel. Then, using the tip of table knife or spatula held just below surface of cream, draw similarly-spaced lines across cake, perpendicular to lines of jam.
- Swirl whipped cream or whipped topping over top of cake. Decorate with chocolate glaze drizzled from tip of iced teaspoon, making series of four or five circles, the first about an inch from edge of cake, the others spaced evenly within.
- Spread lightly sweetened sour cream, whipped cream, or whipped topping on top of cake. Arrange long diagonal slices of banana to form petals of a flower radiating from the center of cake.

Louisiana Sweet Potato Commission

Louisiana Yam Cheesecake (Recipe, p. 165)

LOUISIANA YAM CHEESECAKE
(see photo, p. 164)

Yield: Three 8-inch cakes

Ingredients

GRAHAM CRACKER CRUMBS	1-1/4 quarts
BUTTER *OR* MARGARINE, melted	1/2 pound
GELATINE, UNFLAVORED	6 tablespoons
WATER, cold	1-1/2 cups
EGG YOLKS, beaten	9 (3/4 cup)
SUGAR	1-1/2 cups
SALT	1-1/2 teaspoons
NUTMEG	1-1/2 teaspoons
CINNAMON	1 tablespoon
MILK	1 cup
CREAM CHEESE, softened	3 pounds
VANILLA	1-1/2 tablespoons
YAMS, cooked, mashed	3-3/4 cups
EGG WHITES	9 (1-1/8 cups)
SUGAR	3/4 cup
CREAM, HEAVY	3 cups

Procedure

1. Combine crumbs and butter; mix well. Reserve 3/4 cup for topping. Press remaining crumb mixture over bottom of 3 8-inch spring form pans.

2. Soften gelatine in cold water.

3. Blend egg yolks, first amount of sugar, salt, nutmeg, cinnamon, and milk. Cook, stirring, over low heat until thickened.

4. Add gelatine; stir to dissolve.

5. Add cheese, vanilla, and yams to egg mixture; beat until blended. Chill until mixture mounds when spooned.

6. Beat egg whites until foamy. Add remaining sugar gradually continuing to beat until stiff but not dry.

7. Whip cream. Fold egg whites and cream into yam mixture.

8. Turn into crumb-lined pans. Top with reserved crumbs. Chill until firm.

9. Garnish with additional whipped cream, if desired.

CHEESECAKE

Yield: Four 8-inch cheese cakes

Ingredients

GELATINE, UNFLAVORED	2 ounces
SUGAR	3 cups
SALT	1 tablespoon
EGG YOLKS	8 (2/3 cup)
MILK	1 quart
LEMON PEEL, grated	1/4 cup
COTTAGE CHEESE, CREAMED, sieved	6 pounds (3 quarts)
LEMON JUICE	3/4 cup
VANILLA	2 tablespoons
BUTTER, melted	1/2 cup
SUGAR	1/4 cup
GRAHAM CRACKER CRUMBS	2 cups
CINNAMON	1 teaspoon
NUTMEG	2 teaspoons
EGG WHITES	8 (1 cup)
SALT	1 teaspoon
SUGAR	1 cup
CREAM, HEAVY	1 quart

Procedure

1. Combine the gelatine, first amount of sugar and salt, egg yolks, and milk in top of double boiler; stir to blend well. Cook over simmering water until mixture coats a metal spoon, stirring constantly. Remove from heat.

2. Add lemon peel. Cool.

3. Add cottage cheese, lemon juice, and vanilla. Chill, stirring occasionally, until mixture mounds slightly when dropped from a spoon.

4. While mixture is chilling combine butter, next amount of sugar, graham cracker crumbs, and spices. Set aside.

5. Beat egg whites and remaining salt until foamy. Beat in remaining sugar, 1 tablespoon at a time until stiff peaks form.

6. Whip cream until stiff.

7. Fold beaten egg whites and whipped cream into chilled gelatine mixture.

7. Turn into 4 8-inch spring-form pans. Sprinkle tops with crumb mixture. Chill until firm.

PINEAPPLE CHIFFON CHEESECAKE

Yield: 32 3-ounce portions

Ingredients

GELATIN, LEMON	12 ounces (1-3/4 cups)
SALT	1/4 teaspoon
SUGAR	1/2 cup
HOT WATER AND PINEAPPLE JUICE, to equal	1 quart
LEMON PEEL, grated	1-1/2 tablespoons
COTTAGE CHEESE	3-1/2 cups
EGG WHITES	4 (1/2 cup)
CREAM, HEAVY	1 cup
PINEAPPLE, CANNED, CRUSHED, drained	1-3/4 cups
ZWIEBACK OR GRAHAM CRACKER CRUMBS	2-2/3 cups
SUGAR	1/4 cup
BUTTER, melted	1/4 pound

Procedure

1. Dissolve gelatin, salt, and sugar in hot liquid. Add lemon peel. Cool until slightly thickened.

2. Whip cottage cheese in mixer until smooth. Add slightly thickened gelatin and egg whites to cottage cheese. Whip at medium speed 15 to 20 minutes, or until mixture has doubled in bulk and is fluffy and thick.

3. Whip cream until thick and shiny but not stiff.

4. Fold whipped cream and pineapple into gelatin mixture.

5. Combine crumbs, sugar, and butter. Line pudding pans with two-thirds of the mixture.

6. Pour gelatin mixture over crumbs to a depth of 1-1/4 inches. Cover with remaining crumbs. Chill until firm. Cut in squares.

NO-BAKE PEACH CHEESECAKE

Yield: Four 9-inch cakes

Ingredients

CORN FLAKE CRUMBS	2 quarts (1-1/2 pounds)
SUGAR	1 cup
CINNAMON	1 tablespoon
BUTTER *OR* MARGARINE, melted	8 ounces
CLING PEACH SLICES	1 No. 10 can
PEACH SYRUP	1 cup
CREAM CHEESE, softened	5 pounds
SUGAR, CONFECTIONERS'	3 pounds
LEMON PEEL, grated	2 tablespoons
LEMON JUICE	1/2 cup
GELATINE, UNFLAVORED	2 ounces
WHIPPED CREAM *OR* TOPPING	3 quarts
SOUR CREAM	1 quart

Procedure

1. Blend corn flake crumbs, sugar, and cinnamon. Add butter; mix well.

2. Measure about 2 cups into each 9-inch spring-form pan. Pack tightly on bottom and sides forming a shell.

3. Drain peaches, reserving required amount of syrup.

4. Combine softened cheese, confectioners' sugar, lemon peel, and lemon juice; beat until smooth.

5. Soften gelatine in peach syrup. Dissolve over hot water. Blend into cheese mixture.

6. Add about half of the drained peach slices, reserving rest for garnish. Beat until peaches are "coarsely chopped."

7. Fold in whipped cream.

8. Divide mixture evenly into crumb shells. Chill until firm.

9. Spread each cake with 1 cup sour cream. Garnish with reserved peach slices.

RAISIN POPPYSEED CHEESECAKE TOPPING

Yield: Topping for six 9-inch cheese cakes

Ingredients

RAISINS, SEEDLESS	4-1/2 cups
POPPYSEEDS	1-1/4 cups
SUGAR	3 cups
MILK	3 cups
SALT	1-1/2 teaspoons
BUTTER	6 ounces (3/4 cup)
VANILLA	1 tablespoon
ORANGE PEEL, grated	2 tablespoons
ALMOND EXTRACT	3/4 teaspoon
WALNUTS, finely chopped	1-1/2 cups

Procedure

1. Chop raisins coarsely.
2. Grind poppyseeds to coarse powder in blender or grinder.
3. Combine raisins, poppyseeds, sugar, milk, and salt. Cook over low heat, stirring frequently, 25 to 30 minutes, or until thick.
4. Remove from heat. Stir in butter, vanilla, orange peel, and almond extract. Cool.
5. Add walnuts. Spread on cheese cakes allowing 13-1/2 ounces for each 9-inch cake.

PIES

PIES CONTINUE to carry off honors as one of America's best loved desserts. Imaginative ways of varying pies that come ready-made can increase their dash and produce delightful surprise. Fruit pies take on prestige when presented with a scoop of ice cream, a ladle of sauce, or a wedge of cheese. Other pies, including custard and pumpkin, attract added attention when dressed with a topping, decorative garnish, or glaze.

In many people's estimation, a fruit or mincemeat pie becomes more delectable when served definitely warm. While it is not feasible to hold a pie at this temperature for any length of time, a specialized piece of equipment can reheat the portions when they are ordered.

Cling Peach Advisory Board

Prepared-Ahead Pie with Peach Pinwheel

171

Fruit Pies

TOUCHES TO ADD ORIGINALITY AND SPARKLE

- Sprinkle pie with fine granulated sugar while pie is still warm from oven.
- Dust with confectioners' sugar once cool.
- Ice with thin sugar glaze.

Top with:
Whipped cream, whipped topping
Thick sour cream and a sprinkling of spice
A nut-coated ball of hard sauce (good on a warm pie)

Serve with:
A triangle of mild cheddar, sharp cheddar, gruyere, muenster, or Swiss cheese
Whipped cream cheese
A souffle cup of salted nuts
A small scoop of sharp cheese spread
Creamed cottage cheese

Offer with ice cream:
Vanilla—the all-round favorite
Vanilla with a sprinkling of nutmeg or cinnamon
Butter pecan
Burnt almond
Other companionable flavors

Present with a sauce:
Tart lemon sauce (try with Dutch apple pie)
Warm bourbon or sherry sauce
Nutmeg or cinnamon sauce
Melba sauce (try with peach pie)

Suggested Combinations:

Pie:	*Ice cream:*
Apple	Butter pecan, eggnog, vanilla
Berry	Vanilla with a sprinkling of spice
Cherry	Butter pecan, cherry vanilla, burnt almond
Peach	Lemon, pistachio

Welsh Foods, Inc.

Vanilla Ice Cream—Contrast for Colorful Grape-Cranberry Pie

AVOCADO LIME PIE

Yield: Nine 9-inch pies

Ingredients

CRUSHED PINEAPPLE (WITH SYRUP)	1-1/2 quarts
LIME JUICE	1 cup
WATER, BOILING	as needed
GELATIN, LIME FLAVOR	1-1/2 pounds
SALT	2 teaspoons
AVOCADOS, ripe	3 pounds (4 large)
CREAM CHEESE, softened	1-1/2 pounds
WHIPPED TOPPING MIX, prepared	2 quarts
GRAHAM CRACKER CRUMB CRUSTS, 9-INCH, baked	9

Procedure

1. Drain pineapple, reserving syrup.
2. Add lime juice to syrup. Add enough boiling water to make 1 gallon.
3. Dissolve gelatin and salt in hot liquid. Chill until slightly thickened.
4. Peel avocados; remove stones. Cut half the amount of avocados into small dice.
5. Mash remaining avocados. Add cheese; beat until creamy.
6. Carefully fold in drained pineapple and diced avocados.
7. Fold whipped topping and pineapple mixture into gelatin.
8. Pour into crusts allowing 1 quart per pie. Chill until firm. Garnish with additional topping and thin lime slices, if desired.

JELLIED CHERRY PIE

Yield: 2 gallons (10 9-inch pies)

Ingredients

FROZEN RED CHERRIES, thawed	10 pounds
GELATIN, CHERRY FLAVOR	1-1/2 pounds
	(3-1/2 cups)
SALT	2 teaspoons
WATER, hot	2 quarts
WATER AND CHERRY JUICE,	
cold*	2 quarts
PIE SHELLS, 9-INCH, baked, cooled	10

Procedure

1. Drain cherries. Measure juice: add water to equal required amount.

2. Dissolve gelatin and salt in hot water. Add cold liquid and drained cherries. Chill until slightly thickened.

3. Pour gelatin mixture into baked pie shells, allowing about 3 cups of filling per pie. Chill until firm. Garnish with whipped cream or topping, if desired.

If desired, 1 cup cherry liqueur may be used with the cherry juice; add cold water to make up the required amount of cold liquid.

United Dairy Industry Association

Cointreau-Sauced Fruited Rainbow Pie

EGGNOG APPLE PIE

Yield: Eight 9-inch pies

Ingredients

WHIPPED DESSERT MIX, VANILLA	1 pound, 14 ounces
WATER, cold·	2 quarts
APPLESAUCE, CANNED, chilled	2 quarts
NUTMEG	4 teaspoons
PASTRY PIE SHELLS, 9-INCH, baked	8
WHIPPED TOPPING (optional)	as needed

Procedure

1. Prepare dessert mix with cold water according to package directions.

2. Turn mixer to low speed. Gradually add apple sauce and nutmeg; mix only until blended.

3. Turn into cooled, baked pie shells allowing about 1 quart per pie. Chill until firm.

4. Top with whipped topping, if desired.

FRENCH-STYLE CHERRY PIE

Yield: Five 9-inch pies

Ingredients

MILK, cold	1-1/4 quarts
SOUR CREAM	1-1/2 quarts
ALMOND EXTRACT	1 teaspoon
INSTANT PUDDING, VANILLA	1 No. 2-1/2 can (20–22 ounces)
PIE SHELLS, 9-INCH, baked	5
PIE FILLING, CHERRY, CANNED	1 No. 10 can

Procedure

1. Combine milk, sour cream, and almond extract. Add pudding; stir, or beat at low speed until well blended.

2. Turn into pie shells. Chill 2 hours or until firm.

3. Cut into wedges. Top each portion with canned cherry pie filling.

CHOCOLATE PEAR PIE

Yield: Four 9-inch pies

Ingredients

WHIPPED DESSERT MIX, CHOCOLATE	1 bag
WATER, cold	1 quart
GRAHAM CRACKER CRUSTS 9-INCH, baked, cooled	4
PEAR HALVES, CANNED, chilled, drained, sliced	12
CHOCOLATE SYRUP	1/4 cup

Procedure

1. Blend whipped dessert mix with cold water. Whip at high speed 5 minutes or until light and fluffy.

2. Ladle mixture into crusts allowing about 3-1/2 cups per pie. Chill at least 2 hours.

3. Just before serving, top with pear slices. Drizzle chocolate syrup over top.

BANANA WHIPPED CREAM PIE

Yield: Four 9-inch pies

Ingredients

CREAM, HEAVY	1 quart
SALT	1/4 teaspoon
SUGAR	1/2 cup
VANILLA *OR* ALMOND FLAVORING	1/4 teaspoon
BANANAS, fully ripe	16 to 20
PIE SHELLS, 9-INCH, baked	4
COCONUT, toasted	as needed

Procedure

1. Whip cream and salt; fold in sugar and flavoring.

2. Cover bottom of cooled pie shells with small amount of whipped cream. Peel bananas and slice into pie shells, allowing 4 to 5 bananas per pie. Cover immediately with whipped cream.

3. Garnish with toasted coconut.

Note

A garnish of finely chopped nuts, grated semi-sweet chocolate, or finely chopped candied fruit peel may be used in place of the toasted coconut.

STRAWBERRY GLAZED CHEESE PIE

Yield: Eight 9-inch pies

Ingredients

CREAM CHEESE	5 pounds
SUGAR	2-1/4 pounds
WHIPPED TOPPING MIX	1 12-ounce envelope
GELATIN, STRAWBERRY FLAVOR	1-1/2 pounds
WATER, boiling	2 quarts
STRAWBERRY HALVES, FROZEN, thawed	5 pounds
GRAHAM CRACKER CRUSTS, 9-INCH	8

Procedure

1. Soften cream cheese. Add sugar; beat well.

2. Prepare whipped topping mix according to package directions. Blend into cheese mixture.

3. Dissolve gelatin in boiling water. Cool. Add undrained berries. Chill until slightly thickened.

4. Divide cheese mixture equally into crusts, allowing about 1 quart per pie. Spread, building edges higher than center.

5. Pour slightly thickened gelatin mixture on tops of pies, allowing 2 cups per pie and leaving the narrow rim of filling around edge uncovered with the glaze.

6. Chill until gelatin is set, at least 3 hours.

CRANBERRY FROZEN PIE

Yield: Six 9-inch pies

Ingredients

GRAHAM CRACKER CRUMBS	2-1/4 pounds
SUGAR	1 pound
LEMON PEEL, grated	1/2 cup
BUTTER *OR* MARGARINE, softened	1 pound
WHOLE CRANBERRY SAUCE	6 1-pound cans
LEMON SHERBET	3 quarts

Procedure

1. Combine graham cracker crumbs, sugar, and lemon peel. Add softened butter; blend well, using paddle at low speed for 3 minutes.

2. Remove 3/4 cup of the mixture; set aside.

3. Divide remaining crumb mixture evenly into six 9-inch pie pans; press firmly against bottom and sides using an 8-inch pie pan to press into shape.

4. Spread one can cranberry sauce over bottom of each pie shell. Cover with spoonfuls of sherbet allowing 1 pint of sherbet per pie. Sprinkle tops with reserved crumb mixture.

5. Freeze until firm, about 24 hours.

CHERRY BAVARIAN PIE

Yield: Four 9-inch pies

Ingredients

GELATIN, STRAWBERRY	1 pound
SUGAR	2 cups
WATER, hot	1 quart
RED SOUR CHERRY JUICE	2 cups
RED SOUR CHERRIES (WATER PACK), drained	1 quart
PIE SHELLS, 9-INCH, baked, cooled	4
CREAM, HEAVY	2 cups

Procedure

1. Dissolve gelatin and sugar in hot water. Add cherry juice. Add 1/3 of mixture to cherries.

2. Chill both gelatin mixtures until slightly thickened. Turn the clear gelatin into pie shells. Chill.

3. Whip cream until thick and shiny but not stiff. Fold in cherry mixture. Chill over crushed ice to thicken well. Pour over firm layer in pie shells. Chill.

KEY LIME PIE

Yield: Nine 9-inch pies

Ingredients

GELATIN, LIME FLAVOR	1-1/2 pounds
WATER, boiling	2 quarts
LIME PEEL, grated	1/4 cup
LIME JUICE	1 quart
EGG YOLKS, well beaten	11 ounces (1-1/3 cups)
SWEETENED CONDENSED MILK	8 14-ounce cans
AROMATIC BITTERS	3 tablespoons
WHIPPED TOPPING MIX*	1 12-ounce bag
FOOD COLORING, GREEN	1/8 teaspoon
PIE SHELLS, 9-INCH, baked, cooled	9

Procedure

1. Dissolve gelatin in boiling water. Add lime peel and juice. Slowly pour over beaten egg yolks, beating constantly.

2. Add condensed milk and bitters. Chill until slightly thickened.

3. Prepare topping as directed on bag. Blend in gelatin mixture at low speed of mixer.

4. Add coloring. Pour into pie shells. Chill until firm. Garnish with additional whipped topping, if desired.

If desired, substitute 1 pound (2 cups) egg whites, beaten until stiff, for the whipped topping.

PINEAPPLE PARFAIT PIE

Yield: Six 9-inch pies

Ingredients

PINEAPPLE, CRUSHED	3 pounds
	(1/2 No. 10 can approx.)
PINEAPPLE JUICE AND	
SYRUP, to equal	1-1/2 quarts
GELATIN, LIME FLAVOR	14 ounces
VANILLA ICE CREAM,	
softened until as thick as	
whipped cream or soft ice	
cream	2 quarts
PIE SHELLS, 9-INCH,	
baked, cooled	6

Procedure

1. Drain pineapple, reserving syrup. Add pineapple juice to syrup to make up required amount of liquid. Heat.

2. Dissolve gelatin in hot liquid. Chill over crushed ice until thick as honey.

3. Place on mixer and whip at medium speed about 12 minutes or until mixture has doubled in bulk and is fluffy and thick.

4. Turn mixer to low speed, add softened ice cream and pineapple; mix until just evenly distributed.

5. Turn into baked, cooled pie shells at once, allowing about 3-1/2 cups of filling per pie. Chill until firm. Garnish with whipped cream, or with additional drained crushed pineapple and fresh mint leaves.

Note

If mixture thickens too quickly to handle, warm slightly or stir vigorously.

SPICED TRIFLE PIE

Yield: Four 9-inch pies

Ingredients

VANILLA CREAM PUDDING AND PIE FILLING, prepared	3 quarts
NUTMEG	1 teaspoon
PIE SHELLS, 9-INCH, baked	4
RASPBERRY PRESERVES	1 cup
POUND CAKE CRUMBS	2 cups
CREAM, HEAVY *OR*	3 cups
WHIPPED TOPPING, prepared	1-1/2 quarts
NUTMEG	as needed

Procedure

1. Combine prepared pudding or pie filling with first amount of nutmeg. Spread 1-1/3 cups mixture into bottom of each pie.

2. Spread 1/4 cup preserves evenly over filling in each pie.

3. Scatter 1/2 cup cake crumbs over the preserves in each pie.

4. Cover with remainder of filling, allowing 1-2/3 cups per pie.

5. When using cream, whip until thick and shiny.

6. Spread pies with a thin layer of whipped cream or whipped topping. Pipe a decorative border around edge of each pie.

7. Sprinkle with remaining nutmeg. Chill.

APRICOT GELATIN TARTS A LA MODE

Yield: 3-1/2 quarts filling, 42 tarts, 1/3 cup each

Ingredients

DRIED APRICOT PUREE, unsweetened	1-1/4 quarts
APRICOT JUICE AND WATER, hot, to equal	2 quarts
GELATIN, ORANGE FLAVOR	12 ounces
SALT	1 teaspoon
SUGAR	1-1/2 pounds
TART SHELLS, 3-1/2-INCH, baked, cooled	42
ICE CREAM, VANILLA	1 gallon

Procedure

1. For apricot puree, cook 1-3/4 pounds dried apricots in water to cover, until tender. Drain, reserving juice. Put drained apricots through sieve or food mill.

2. Measure apricot juice; add water to make required amount. Heat.

3. Dissolve gelatin, salt, and sugar in the hot liquid. Add apricot puree; chill until slightly thickened.

4. Turn into baked tart shells allowing 1/3 cup per tart. Chill until firm. Serve topped with a No. 20 scoop of ice cream.

PRUNE CREAM TARTS

Yield: 24 tarts

Ingredients

VANILLA PUDDING AND PIE FILLING, cooked, chilled	2 quarts
ALMOND EXTRACT	1 teaspoon
PRUNES, cooked, pitted, chopped	3 cups
SUGAR, BROWN	1/2 cup
LEMON PEEL, grated	1 tablespoon
LEMON JUICE	3 tablespoons
INDIVIDUAL TART SHELLS, baked	24
WHIPPED CREAM	as needed
ALMONDS, slivered, toasted	1/2 cup

Procedure

1. Combine chilled pudding and almond extract.

2. Combine prunes, brown sugar, lemon peel, and juice. Mix well.

3. Divide prune mixture into tart shells. Spoon pudding over prunes allowing 1/3 cup per tart. Chill.

4. Decorate with whipped cream; sprinkle with almonds.

Pumpkin Pie

ADD ORIGINALITY AND SPARKLE to pumpkin pie with nut garnish or glaze or other dress-up touches. If nuts are part of the plan, sprinkle them over the pie about 10 minutes before it is done. See also Pumpkin Chiffon Pie, page 203.

Glaze with:

Orange Glaze (see recipe for Orange Glazed Pumpkin Pie, page 187)

Sour Cream-Nut Glaze (recipe page 282)

Sprinkle with:

Slivered almonds

Pecan halves

Chopped walnuts

Peanuts

Filberts

Serve with:

Whipped cream or whipped topping sweetened and flavored with honey, molasses, or brown sugar

Sour cream

Lemon-Sour Cream Topping (recipe page 264)

A wedge of cheddar cheese

Whipped cream cheese and chopped nuts

Vanilla ice cream with a sprinkling of cinnamon

ORANGE GLAZED PUMPKIN* PIE

Yield: Three 9-inch pies

Ingredients

SUGAR	3/4 cup
CORNSTARCH	1/3 cup
SALT	1/8 teaspoon
WATER	3/4 cup
ORANGE PEEL, grated	6 tablespoons
ORANGE JUICE	2 cups
PUMPKIN PIES, 9-INCH, baked	3
CREAM, HEAVY	1-1/2 cups
ORANGE SECTIONS	as needed

Procedure

1. Combine sugar, cornstarch, and salt.

2. Gradually add water, orange peel, and juice.

3. Cook, stirring over medium heat, until thickened. Continue to cook for 5 minutes. Cool slightly.

4. While warm, spread over baked pumpkin (or custard) pies allowing 10 ounces per pie.

5. Whip cream. Garnish each wedge of pie with whipped cream and an orange section.

*or Custard

Custard Pies

ALLOW CUSTARD PIES to cool completely. Then serve plain or vary the presentation with a glaze, garnish, or topping.

Glaze with:

Berry Glaze (recipe page 280)

Sour Cream-Nut Glaze (recipe page 282)

Orange Glaze (see recipe for Orange Glazed Pumpkin Pie, page 187)

Serve with:

Honey Whipped Cream (recipe page 276)

Lemon-Sour Cream Topping (recipe page 264)

Pecan Pie

- *Top with unsweetened whipped cream or whipped topping.*
- *Garnish with pecan halves.*
- *Serve with vanilla ice cream.*

PEACH PECAN PIE

Yield: Five 9-inch pies

Ingredients

EGGS, BEATEN	1-1/4 pounds
PIE FILLING, PEACH	1 No. 10 can
SALT	3/4 teaspoon
CORN SYRUP, DARK	2 pounds, 13 ounces
PECAN HALVES	1 pound
VANILLA	4 teaspoons
PASTRY SHELLS, 9-INCH, unbaked	5

Procedure

1. Beat eggs until light.
2. Stir in pie filling and salt.
3. Add corn syrup, pecans, and vanilla; blend.
4. Scale 2-1/4 pounds into each unbaked pastry shell.
5. Bake in oven at 425°F. for 10 minutes. Reduce heat to 325°F. Bake 45 to 50 minutes, until filling is set.

CHOCOLATE PRALINE PIE

Yield: Four 9-inch pies

Ingredients

BUTTER *OR* MARGARINE	11 ounces
SUGAR, BROWN	8 ounces
PECANS, chopped	8 ounces
PIE SHELLS, 9-INCH, lightly baked	4
WHIPPED DESSERT MIX, CHOCOLATE	15 ounces
WATER, cold	1 quart

Procedure

1. Combine butter and sugar in saucepan. Cook, stirring, until sugar melts and mixture bubbles.
2. Remove from heat; stir in nuts. Spread over bottoms of pie shells.
3. Bake in oven at 425°F. 5 minutes or until bubbly. Cool.
4. Blend dessert mix with cold water. Whip at high speed 5 minutes, or until light and fluffy.
5. Ladle into pie shells, allowing about 3-1/2 cups per pie. Chill at least 4 hours.

Mincemeat Pie

Serve warm with

Whipped cream or whipped topping

    sweetened with brown sugar (Amber Whipped Cream, recipe, page 276, Amber Topping recipe, page 277

    flavored with rum or brandy

    decorated with grated orange peel

Brandy, rum, or sherry sauce

Orange- or lemon-flavored Sunshine sauce

Foamy sauce

Hard sauce

    flavored with sherry, rum, or brandy

    garnished with chopped nuts or raisins

Sharp cheddar cheese (cubes, wedges, or grated)

Whipped cream cheese

Vanilla, coffee, eggnog, or rum-raisin ice cream

ICE CREAM PIE WITH MINCEMEAT SAUCE

Yield: Six 9-inch pies

Ingredients

GRAHAM CRACKER CRUMBS (FINE)	2-1/4 pounds
BUTTER *OR* MARGARINE, softened to room temperature	1 pound
SUGAR	1 pound
ICE CREAM, VANILLA *OR* COFFEE	1-1/2 gallons

Procedure

1. Prepare fine graham cracker crumbs using grinder attachment of mixer. Or, use ready-prepared crumbs.

2. Combine crumbs, softened butter, and sugar; blend thoroughly on mixer, using paddle at low speed for 3 minutes.

3. Divide mixture into 9-inch pie pans; press firmly against bottom and sides of pan using an 8-inch pie pan to press crumbs into shape.

4. For unbaked crusts: chill thoroughly before filling. For baked crusts: Bake in oven at 375°F. for 8 minutes.

5. Fill well-chilled baked or unbaked crumb crusts with slightly softened vanilla or coffee ice cream allowing 1 quart per pie. Freeze until firm.

6. Serve with Mincemeat Sauce. See following recipe.

MINCEMEAT SAUCE

Yield: 1-1/2 gallons, 96 1/4-cup portions

Ingredients

GELATIN, LEMON *OR* CHERRY FLAVOR	12 ounces (1-3/4 cups)
WATER, hot, (140°-160°F.)	3 quarts
MINCEMEAT, prepared	8 pounds (3 quarts)
BRANDY (optional)	1-1/2 cups

Procedure

1. Dissolve gelatin in hot water. Add mincemeat and brandy.

2. Chill until slightly thickened.

Specialty Pies

THESE ARE EXAMPLES of pies that stand out as "different." They command attention and win a following with an intriguing name as well as ravishing appearance and promising taste.

FROZEN COFFEE BAVARIAN PIE

Yield: Five 9-inch pies

Ingredients

WHIPPED TOPPING MIX	12 ounces
SUGAR, BROWN	6 to 8 ounces
SOLUBLE COFFEE	1/4 to 1/3 cup
VANILLA	1 tablespoon
WATER	3-3/4 cups
PECANS, chopped	1 cup
PIE SHELLS, 9-INCH, baked, cooled	5

Procedure

1. Combine topping mix, brown sugar, soluble coffee, vanilla, and water in 20-quart mixer bowl. Mix well on low speed; whip at high speed 5 to 8 minutes, or until topping forms soft peaks.

2. Fold in pecans. Ladle into pie shells, allowing about 1 quart per pie. Freeze until firm.

3. Garnish with additional prepared whipped topping and pecans, if desired.

SODA CRACKER PIE

Yield: Four 9-inch pies

Ingredients

SODA CRACKERS	1/2 pound
NUTMEATS, finely chopped	12 ounces
CREAM OF TARTAR	1 teaspoon
EGG WHITES	2 cups
SUGAR	1-1/4 pounds
VANILLA	4 teaspoons

Procedure

1. Roll soda crackers or put through grinder to make fine crumbs. Mix with nuts.

2. Add cream of tartar to egg whites; beat until foamy. Add sugar gradually, continuing to beat until stiff; fold in cracker mixture and vanilla.

3. Spread into four greased 9-inch pie pans. Bake in oven at 350°F. 30 minutes. Cool.

4. Serve topped with ice cream.

MARGARITA PIE

Yield: Four 9-inch pies

Ingredients

PRETZEL CRUMBS, finely crushed	3 cups
SUGAR	2/3 cup
BUTTER *OR* MARGARINE, melted	1-1/3 cups
GELATINE, UNFLAVORED	3 tablespoons
LEMON PEEL, grated	1 tablespoon
LEMON JUICE, freshly squeezed	1-1/4 cups
EGG YOLKS	1 cup
SUGAR	1-1/2 cups
SALT	3/4 teaspoon
TEQUILA	6 ounces
TRIPLE SEC	3 ounces
EGG WHITES	2 cups
SUGAR	1-1/4 cups
LEMONS, thinly sliced	3 to 4

Procedure

1. Combine crumbs and first amount of sugar; add butter, mixing well.

2. Reserve 1/2 cup crumbs for garnish. Press 1 cup of remaining crumbs into each of 4 well-buttered pie pans to form shells. Chill.

3. Combine gelatine, lemon peel, and lemon juice; let stand 5 minutes.

4. Beat egg yolks until thick: beat in next amount of sugar and salt. Add gelatine mixture. Cook, stirring, over hot water until slightly thickened and gelatine is dissolved.

5. Remove from heat; immediately blend in liqueurs. Chill over ice water until cool.

6. Beat egg whites just to soft peak stage; gradually beat in remaining sugar at high speed.

7. Carefully fold yolk mixture (about 1/3 at a time) into whites.

8. Turn into pie shells. Chill until set. Garnish with reserved pretzel mixture and lemon cartwheel twists.

STRAWBERRY DAIQUIRI PIE
(pictured on cover, central inset)

Yield: Four 9-inch pies

Ingredients

GRAHAM CRACKER CRUMBS	1-1/2 quarts
SUGAR	1 cup
NUTS, finely chopped	1 cup
BUTTER *OR* MARGARINE, melted	1-1/3 cups
GELATINE, UNFLAVORED	1/4 cup
WATER	1 cup
STRAWBERRIES, FRESH, sliced, to equal	2 quarts
SUGAR	2 cups
LIME JUICE	1 cup
RUM EXTRACT	1/4 cup
EGG WHITES	2 cups
CREAM OF TARTAR	1 teaspoon
SUGAR	1-1/3 cups
WHIPPED TOPPING, prepared	2 cups
WHIPPED TOPPING, prepared	1-1/2 quarts
STRAWBERRIES, FRESH, WHOLE*	2 cups

Procedure

1. Combine graham cracker crumbs, first amount of sugar, and nuts. Add melted butter; mix.

2. Press 2 cups crumb mixture into each pie pan to form shells. Bake in oven at 400°F. for 8 minutes. Cool.

3. Soften gelatine in water.

4. Partially crush sliced strawberries, add second amount of sugar.

5. Bring to a boil. Add softened gelatine to hot strawberry mixture; stir until gelatine is dissolved.

6. Cool slightly. Add lime juice and rum extract. Chill until mixture mounds slightly when dropped from spoon.

7. Beat egg whites and cream of tartar until foamy. Gradually beat in remaining sugar; continue to beat until stiff and glossy.

8. Fold chilled strawberry mixture into beaten egg whites. Gently fold in first amount of whipped topping.

9. Turn into pie shells. Chill until set, allowing at least 3 hours.

10. Garnish with remaining whipped topping and the whole berries.

A 40-ounce package of thawed, frozen, sliced strawberries may be substituted. If so, omit second amount of sugar and step 4.

IRISH WHISKEY PIE

Yield: Four 10-inch pies

Ingredients

GELATINE, UNFLAVORED	1/3 cup
IRISH WHISKEY	1-1/4 cups
MILK	1/2 gallon
NUTMEG, GROUND	2 teaspoons
SUGAR	2-2/3 cups
EGG YOLKS, well beaten	16 (1-1/3 cups)
SALT	1 tablespoon
CREAM, HEAVY*	1 quart
GREEN FOOD COLORING	as needed
GREEN MARASCHINO CHERRIES, chopped, well drained	1 quart
PIE SHELLS, 10-INCH, baked	4

Procedure

1. Sprinkle gelatine over whiskey to soften.
2. Combine milk, nutmeg, and sugar; heat to just below boiling point.
3. Blend a small amount of milk mixture into egg yolks; return to milk mixture. Cook over low heat, stirring constantly, until mixture coats a metal spoon.
4. Add salt and gelatine; stir until gelatine is completely dissolved.
5. Chill until mixture mounds when spooned.
6. Whip cream; fold into gelatine mixture. Add green coloring to tint a pale green. Fold in chopped cherries.
7. Turn into baked pie shells. Chill until firm.

Or, 2 quarts prepared whipped topping.

Chiffon Pies

LIGHT AND LUSCIOUS, chiffon pies boast both eye and taste appeal. The delights of these pies start with their crisp crusts—pastry or crumb—and continue in their light, daintily flavored fillings.

A boon to the busy kitchen, these pies can be prepared ahead and held in the refrigerator, ready to cut and serve. Ready-made pie shells help save time, while unbaked crumb shells rule out the need for an oven.

Whipped cream or whipped topping is one of the most popular finishes for chiffon pies. Swirled across the top or arranged in an attractive border, it often suffices as both topping and garnish.

Sprinkle-on garnishes such as plain, toasted, or tinted coconut, crushed candy, grated chocolate, and finely chopped nuts can enhance a chiffon pie. Another very simple idea is to add crumb mixture reserved from the crust as a garnish to the completed pie.

Berries, pieces of fruit, mint leaves, chocolate curls, or drizzles of chocolate glaze make other decorative garnishes for chiffon pies. A lemon chiffon pie gains interest when garnished with mint leaves and small clusters of frosted white grapes. Similarly, a pink peppermint chiffon makes a striking picture when finished with a lacy network of chocolate glaze. Try garnish ideas from this book or create your own to complement the chiffon pies you serve.

PEANUT BUTTER BANANA CHIFFON PIE

Yield: Five 9-inch pies

Ingredients

GELATINE, UNFLAVORED	1/4 cup
WATER, cold	2 cups
SUGAR	2/3 cup
PEANUT BUTTER, SMOOTH OR CRUNCHY	2-1/2 cups
NUTMEG	2 teaspoons
WATER	3 cups
EGG YOLKS, beaten	12 (1 cup)
VANILLA	1-1/2 tablespoons
EGG WHITES	12 (1-1/2 cups)
SUGAR	2/3 cup
BANANAS, LARGE, ripe	5
PIE SHELLS, 9-INCH, baked	5
CREAM, HEAVY	2-1/2 cups

Procedure

1. Soak gelatine in cold water 5 minutes.

2. Combine first amount of sugar, peanut butter, nutmeg, and water; blend. Add beaten egg yolks.

3. Cook, beating with wire whip, until mixture is thick. Beat in softened gelatine and vanilla. Chill until slightly thickened.

4. Beat egg whites until foamy. Add remaining sugar gradually, continuing to beat until stiff. Fold into gelatine mixture.

5. Slice a banana into the bottom of each pie shell. Add chiffon mixture. Chill until firm.

6. Whip cream; sweeten, if desired. Spread on pies.

PEPPERMINT CHIFFON PIE

Yield: Five 9-inch pies

Ingredients	
GELATINE, UNFLAVORED	1-1/2 ounces
MILK, cold	2 cups
MILK, hot	1-1/4 quarts
SUGAR	3/4 cup
SALT	1/2 teaspoon
EGG YOLKS	12 (1 cup)
PEPPERMINT FLAVORING	3/4 teaspoon
EGG WHITES	12 (1-1/2 cups)
SUGAR	1 cup
CREAM, HEAVY	2-1/2 cups
PEPPERMINT CANDY, CRUSHED	2 cups
RED COLORING (OPTIONAL)	as needed
CHOCOLATE COOKIE CRUMB CRUSTS, 9-INCH	5

Procedure

1. Soak gelatine in cold milk 5 minutes. Add to hot milk; stir until gelatine is dissolved.

2. Add first amount of sugar and salt; blend.

3. Beat egg yolks well. Add hot gelatine mixture, stirring to blend thoroughly. Cool.

4. Add peppermint flavoring. Chill until slightly thickened.

5. Beat egg whites until foamy throughout. Add remaining sugar gradually, beating until mixture forms glossy peaks. Do not overbeat.

6. Fold slightly thickened gelatine mixture into meringue.

7. Whip cream until thick and shiny but not stiff. Fold whipped cream and crushed candy into gelatine mixture. Add red coloring to give desired pink shade.

8. Turn into crumb crusts. Chill until firm. Finish top with drizzles of Chocolate Glaze. (See recipe, page 280)

International Apple Institute

Imaginative Garnish for Apple Chiffon Pie

LEMON CHIFFON PIE

Yield: Nine 8-inch pies

Ingredients

GELATINE, UNFLAVORED	1/2 cup
SUGAR	1-1/4 quarts
SALT	4 teaspoons
WATER, boiling	2 cups
EGG YOLKS	24 (2 cups)
LEMON JUICE	1 quart
LEMON PEEL, grated	1/4 cup
EGG WHITES	24 (3 cups)
SUGAR	2-2/3 cups
PIE SHELLS, 8-INCH, baked	9
CREAM, HEAVY	3 cups

Procedure

1. Mix gelatine, first amount of sugar and salt together thoroughly in saucepan. Add boiling water; heat, stirring, until sugar and gelatine dissolve.

2. Beat egg yolks until thick; beat in lemon juice gradually; add lemon peel.

3. Blend egg yolk mixture into hot gelatine and sugar mixture. Chill until mixture mounds when dropped from a spoon.

4. Beat egg whites, add remaining sugar gradually, continue beating until stiff and shiny. Fold into chilled mixture.

5. Turn into cold, baked pie shells; chill until firm.

6. Whip cream. Spread over tops of pies or pipe whipped cream around edge as a border.

ORANGE CHIFFON PIE

Yield: Eight 9-inch pies

Ingredients

GELATINE, UNFLAVORED	1/2 cup
WATER, cold	2 cups
EGG YOLKS, beaten	32 (2-2/3 cups)
SUGAR	1 quart
SALT	2 teaspoons
ORANGE PEEL, grated	3 tablespoons
ORANGE JUICE	1 quart
LEMON JUICE	1/2 cup
EGG WHITES	32 (1 quart)
SUGAR	2 cups
PIE SHELLS, baked	8
CREAM, WHIPPED	2-1/2 quarts

Procedure

1. Soak gelatine in cold water; dissolve over hot water.

2. Combine egg yolks, first amount of sugar, and salt in double boiler. Cook over simmering water until mixture coats a spoon, stirring constantly. Add softened gelatine; stir until dissolved.

3. Add orange peel, orange juice, and lemon juice to custard mixture; chill until slightly thickened.

4. Beat egg whites until foamy throughout. Add remaining sugar gradually; beat until stiff peaks form.

5. Fold gelatine mixture into meringue. Fill cooled pie shells. Chill until set.

6. Spread thin layer of whipped cream over pie tops. Pipe a border around edge with pastry tube.

PUMPKIN CHIFFON PIE

Yield: 9 quarts filling for 10 9-inch pies, 3-1/2 cups filling per pie

Ingredients

GELATINE, UNFLAVORED	2-1/2 ounces (1/2 cup)
MILK, cold	2 cups
MILK, hot	1-3/4 quarts
SUGAR, BROWN	1 pound
SALT	2 tablespoons
CINNAMON	4 teaspoons
NUTMEG	2 teaspoons
GINGER	2 teaspoons
EGG YOLKS	18 (1-1/2 cups)
PUMPKIN	3-1/2 cups
EGG WHITES	18 (2-1/4 cups)
GRANULATED SUGAR	2-1/2 cups
CREAM, HEAVY	2 cups
PIE SHELLS, 9-INCH, baked	10

Procedure

1. Soak gelatine in cold milk 5 minutes. Add hot milk; stir until gelatine is dissolved.

2. Add brown sugar, salt, and spices; blend.

3. Beat egg yolks. Pour warm gelatine mixture over yolks, stirring well. Add pumpkin; blend. Chill until slightly thickened.

4. Beat egg whites until foamy throughout. Add granulated sugar gradually continuing to beat until mixture stands in soft peaks. Fold in slightly thickened pumpkin mixture.

5. Whip cream until thick and shiny but not stiff. Fold into pumpkin mixture.

6. Turn into cooled pie shells, allowing 3-1/2 cups filling per shell. Chill until firm. Garnish with sweetened, whipped cream and sprinkle lightly with cinnamon, if desired.

EGGNOG CHIFFON PIE

Yield: Five 9-inch pies

Ingredients

GELATINE, PLAIN	1-1/2 ounces
MILK, cold	2 cups
MILK, hot	1 quart
SUGAR	3/4 cup
SALT	1/2 teaspoon
EGG YOLKS	10 (7 ounces)
NUTMEG	1/2 teaspoon
SHERRY WINE	1 cup
EGG WHITES	10 (10 ounces)
SUGAR	1 cup
CREAM, HEAVY	2-1/2 cups
PIE SHELLS, 9-INCH, baked	5

Procedure

1. Soak gelatine in cold milk 5 minutes. Add hot milk; stir until gelatine is dissolved. Add first amount of sugar and salt; blend.

2. Beat egg yolks well. Add warm gelatine mixture, stirring well. Cool.

3. Add nutmeg and sherry. Chill until slightly thickened.

4. Beat egg whites until foamy throughout. Add remaining sugar gradually and continue beating until mixture stands in soft peaks. Fold in slightly thickened gelatine mixture.

5. Whip cream until thick and shiny, but not stiff. Fold into gelatine mixture.

6. Turn into cooled pie shells, allowing 1 quart of filling per pie. Chill until firm. Garnish with macaroon crumbs or with sweetened whipped cream and chopped maraschino cherries.

PEACH-TOPPED LEMONADE CHIFFON PIE

Yield: Six 9-inch pies

Ingredients

EGG YOLKS	24 (2 cups)
WATER	3 cups
SALT	1 teaspoon
GELATINE, UNFLAVORED	1-1/2 ounces
LEMONADE CONCENTRATE, FROZEN	6 6-ounce cans
EGG WHITES	24 (3 cups)
SUGAR	3 cups
PIE SHELLS, (PASTRY OR CRUMB) baked, cooled	6 9-inch
PEACH SLICES, FRESH, FROZEN OR CANNED	as needed

Procedure

1. Beat egg yolks with water; add salt.

2. Sprinkle gelatine over top of mixture. Place over low heat; stir constantly until gelatine dissolves and mixture thickens slightly.

3. Remove from heat; add frozen lemonade concentrate. Stir until melted.

4. If necessary, chill, stirring occasionally, until mixture mounds slightly when dropped from spoon.

5. Beat egg whites until stiff but not dry. Gradually add sugar, continuing to beat until stiff peaks form.

6. Fold in gelatine mixture. Turn into baked, cooled pie shells. Chill until firm.

7. Serve topped with drained peach slices.

STRAWBERRY CHIFFON PIE

Yield: 60 9-inch pies

Ingredients

STRAWBERRIES, FROZEN (5 TO 1 PACK)	30 pounds
JUICE FROM STRAWBERRIES	1-1/2 quarts
SUGAR	5 pounds
SALT	2-1/2 ounces
CORNSTARCH	2 pounds 10 ounces
GELATINE, UNFLAVORED	5 ounces
WATER	1-1/2 quarts
EGG WHITES	1-1/4 gallons
SUGAR	5 pounds
SUGAR	2-1/2 pounds
GRAHAM CRACKER PIE SHELLS, 9-INCH	60

Procedure

1. Defrost berries, take off required amount of juice. Combine berries (and all the remaining juice) with first amount of sugar and salt; bring to a boil.

2. Blend cornstarch and gelatine with water and the reserved strawberry juice. Add slowly to hot berry mixture; cook, stirring, until clear.

3. Beat egg whites with second amount of sugar until stiff. Add remaining sugar, beat one more minute.

4. Add hot cornstarch mixture; mix carefully, but well.

5. Fill pie shells allowing generous 3/4 quart filling per pie. Refrigerate.

Note

Pies freeze successfully.

GELATIN DESSERTS

MANY GELATIN DESSERTS are simple affairs; they need few ingredients, and are child's play to prepare. Happily, they are also designed to be made in advance. Among the favorites in light desserts, gelatin desserts are modest in calories and low in cost. As if that weren't all, there are time-saving tips as well as a bundle of tricks for making them showier and giving them sales appeal.

Made with unflavored gelatine according to recipe, or with fruit-flavored gelatin following package directions, clear sparkling jelled desserts have the kind of versatility that knows few rivals. The character changes miraculously with a mere change in form. Gelatin cut into cubes is quite different. It can also be flaked, whipped, or layered, as well as turned out in attractive and varied molds.

One of the first rules to ensure a clear, uniformly set jelly is to be certain that the gelatine dissolves completely. With the unflavored product, begin by sprinkling it on the surface of a small amount of cold water or other cold liquid. Heat the remainder of the liquid; add the softened gelatine, and stir until dissolved.

While fruit-flavored gelatins require no soaking, the dissolving step is no less important. Have the liquid very hot—nearly boiling—add it to the gelatin, and stir long enough to get every bit of the gelatin into solution.

When haste is required, the setting process can be speeded by using the ice and water method. Simply measure one-third of the liquid called for to dissolve the gelatin. (Or up to one-half if that makes an easier measurement.) Bring this amount to a boil; add to the gelatin; stir until dissolved. Measure the rest of the required liquid using crushed ice; add cold water just to cover the ice in the measuring container. Add to the

207

dissolved gelatin, stirring until the ice melts and the gelatin thickens. Avoid any brisk stirring after the thickening begins, as this can entrap air bubbles and mar the clear, sparkling look.

TO MAKE GELATIN CUBES

Pour dissolved gelatin 1/2 to 3/4 inch deep in shallow pans. When firm, cut into cubes, using a knife dipped in hot water.
  To vary the service:

- Pile cubes of one flavor in a serving dish.
- Combine two or more flavors, jumbling the colors or arranging in layers.
- Mix gelatin cubes with strawberry halves and/or other fruits.
- Arrange cubes with vanilla pudding or whipped topping, alternating layers in a tall parfait glass.

TO MAKE GELATIN FLAKES

Run firmly set gelatin through the grinder, using the medium blade with the machine at high speed. Only one word of caution: be sure the grinder parts are cold.
  To vary the service:

- Feature with unwhipped cream or custard sauce.
- Top with ice cream, whipped cream, whipped topping, pieces of fruit, or a sprinkle of coconut.
- Dish two colors side by side in a flat nappy or sherbet dish.
- Arrange a rainbow of assorted colors by layering in a tall serving glass.

TO WHIP GELATIN

Chill gelatin until slightly thickened, about the consistency of honey or unbeaten egg white. Turn into a chilled mixer bowl; whip at medium speed until thick and fluffy and doubled in bulk. Chill over crushed ice, stirring occasionally, until gelatin mounds when spooned.

To vary the service:

- Pour into molds or a shallow pan; complete the setting; unmold or cut into squares.
- Fold in fruit or cubes of gelatin before turning into serving dishes, molds, or pans for setting.
- Present with whipped cream, whipped topping, fruit, or custard sauce.

TO LAYER GELATIN

Chill each layer until set, but not quite firm, before adding the next.

To vary the service:

- Mold a series of various colored layers on a slant. To do this, catch the base of stemmed serving glasses between the bars of the refrigerator rack and lean the glasses against the wall of the refrigerator. Pour gelatin into tilted glass; allow to set undisturbed. Repeat with different colored gelatin until glasses are full.
- Mold a single layer of clear gelatin, slanted or level, in a stemmed glass. When set, fill the glass with whipped gelatin with whipped topping folded in.
- Alternate layers of partially set gelatin with whipped topping, chill the portions to complete the setting.

TO MOLD GELATIN

Fill individual molds to brim; unmold when firm. Gelatin is firm enough to unmold when top isn't sticky and gelatin doesn't sag when mold is tilted.

To vary the service:

- Place the unmolded portion of gelatin in a glass nappie containing a ladle of custard sauce or crushed, sweetened berries.

- Surround the base of the unmolded gelatin with a ruffle of whipped topping.
- Pour 1/2 inch of clear gelatin into mold. Chill. Fill with whipped gelatin of the same flavor.
- Mold clear gelatin in a ring mold. Fill center of unmolded ring with flaked gelatin, halved strawberries, or other fruit.

United Dairy Industry Association

Fresh Strawberry Pie a la Mode

Jellied Desserts

JELLIED GINGER MOLD

Yield: 24 portions

Ingredients

GELATIN, ORANGE FLAVOR	12 ounces
GINGERALE, hot	1 quart
ORANGE JUICE, FRESH OR FROZEN RECONSTITUTED	1 quart

Procedure

1. Dissolve gelatin in hot gingerale. Add orange juice; chill until slightly thickened.
2. Whip until thick and fluffy and double in bulk.
3. Turn into individual molds. Or, for buffet service turn into two 2-quart ring molds. Chill until firm.
4. Unmold; serve with strawberries, or orange sections and sour cream.

WINE JELLY

Yield: 32 portions

Ingredients

GELATINE, UNFLAVORED	2 ounces
WATER, cold	2 cups
WATER, boiling	1 quart
SUGAR	2-2/3 cups
SALT	1/4 teaspoon
LEMON JUICE, strained	1 cup
ORANGE JUICE, strained	1 cup
SHERRY WINE	2 quarts

Procedure

1. Soften gelatine in cold water.
2. Dissolve in boiling water. Add remaining ingredients; blend well.
3. Pour into individual molds or in shallow pans; chill until firm.
4. Unmold or cut into squares: Serve with sour cream.

211

FRUIT-WINE JELLY

Yield: 24 portions

Ingredients

CHIANTI WINE	1-1/4 quarts
ORANGE SECTIONS	1-1/4 quarts
GELATIN, RASPBERRY FLAVOR	1 pound (2-1/3 cups)
WATER, hot	1-1/4 quarts
CREAM, HEAVY	2 cups
SUGAR, CONFECTIONERS'	1/2 cup

Procedure

1. Pour wine over oranges, allow to stand 30 minutes.
2. Dissolve gelatin in hot water. Cool. Add orange and wine mixture. Chill until slightly thickened.
3. Turn into sherbet glasses or individual molds. Chill until firm.
4. Whip cream; add sugar.
5. Serve jelly garnished with sweetened whipped cream.

CREAMY VANILLA SAUCE
(delicious on Jellied Orange Ambrosia, recipe page 217)

Yield: 1 gallon

Ingredients

PIE FILLING AND PUDDING, VANILLA	14 ounces (2 cups)
MILK, cold	2 cups
MILK, scalded	3-1/2 quarts
SUGAR	1 cup

Procedure

1. Mix pudding powder with cold milk. Add to hot milk; add sugar.
2. Cook over boiling water, stirring constantly until mixture thickens, about 3 minutes. Then cook 10 minutes longer, stirring often. Remove from heat. Chill.

GRASSHOPPER DESSERT

Yield: 3 gallons (100 portions)

Ingredients

GELATIN, LIME FLAVOR	3 pounds
SUGAR	1 cup
WATER, hot	1-3/4 gallons
CREME DE MENTHE LIQUEUR	2 cups
WHIPPED TOPPING MIX	12 ounces
WATER, ice-cold	1 quart
WHIPPED TOPPING MIX	12 ounces
WATER, ice-cold	3 cups
CREME DE CACAO LIQUEUR, chilled	1 cup

Procedure

1. Dissolve gelatin and sugar in hot water. Stir in Creme de Menthe.

2. Pour 3 quarts of gelatin mixture in shallow pans to depth of 1/2 inch. Chill until firm. Chill remaining gelatin until slightly thickened.

3. Prepare first amount of whipped topping with water as directed on package.

4. At low speed of mixer, fold slightly thickened gelatin into whipped topping.

5. Pour into serving bowls or individual dessert dishes, filling three-quarts full. Chill until firm.

6. Cut pans of clear gelatin into cubes. Arrange on top of desserts.

7. Prepare remaining amount of whipped topping with water and liqueur as directed on package. Use as topping for dessert.

8. Garnish with chocolate curls and fresh mint, if desired.

GRASSHOPPER PARFAIT

Yield: 48 portions, 1/2 cup gelatin, 3 tablespoons cream

Ingredients

GELATIN, LIME FLAVOR	2-1/4 pounds (5-1/4 cups)
SALT	3/4 teaspoon
WATER, hot	5-1/2 quarts
CREME DE MENTHE, GREEN	2 cups
CREAM, HEAVY	1 quart
CREME DE MENTHE, GREEN, chilled	3/4 cup
CREME DE CACAO, WHITE OR BROWN, chilled	3/4 cup

Procedure

1. Dissolve gelatin and salt in hot water. Cool.

2. Add first amount of Creme de Menthe. Turn into shallow pans. Chill until firm.

3. Force firmly set gelatin through a chilled ricer, or run through the grinder using medium blade at high speed. (Have grinder parts cold.)

4. Whip cream until smooth and shiny. Gradually add remaining Creme de Menthe and Creme de Cacao, whipping at medium speed to soft peaks.

5. To serve, alternate layers of gelatin flakes and cream mixture in parfaits.

Speedy and Simple Gelatin Desserts

ORANGE-DATE MOLD

Yield: 50 portions

Ingredients

ORANGE SECTIONS from	10 oranges
DATES, pitted, chopped	2 pounds
ORANGE JUICE	1-1/2 cups
LEMON JUICE	1/2 cup
GELATIN, ORANGE FLAVOR	1-1/2 pounds (3-1/2 cups)
SALT	1 teaspoon
SUGAR	1 cup
HOT WATER	3-1/2 quarts
PECANS, coarsely chopped	2 cups

Procedure

1. Combine orange sections, chopped dates, and orange and lemon juices; let stand 30 minutes.

2. Combine gelatin, salt, and sugar; dissolve in hot water. Chill until slightly thickened.

3. Fold fruit mixture and nuts into gelatin. Pour into individual molds or into shallow pans.

4. Chill until set. Unmold or cut into squares. Garnish with whipped cream or topping, if desired.

HOLIDAY MINCEMEAT MOLD

Yield: 4-1/2 quarts, approximately 48 portions

Ingredients

GELATIN, LEMON FLAVOR	1-1/2 pounds
PINEAPPLE JUICE, hot	2—46-ounce cans
MINCEMEAT, CANNED	2 quarts

Procedure

1. Dissolve gelatin in hot pineapple juice. Chill until partially thickened.

2. Fold in mincemeat. Pour into shallow pans or into large or individual molds. Chill until firm.

3. Garnish with whipped cream or topping and a sprinkling of chopped nuts or diced candied fruits, if desired.

JELLIED ORANGE AMBROSIA

Yield: 48 1/2-cup portions

Ingredients

ORANGE SECTIONS	1-1/2 quarts
GELATIN, ORANGE FLAVOR	1-1/2 pounds (3-1/2 cups)
SALT	1 teaspoon
WATER, boiling	1-1/2 quarts
CRUSHED ICE, JUICE, AND WATER	2 quarts
ORANGE PEEL, grated	2 tablespoons
BANANAS, sliced	2 pounds (1-1/2 quarts)
COCONUT	8 ounces (3 cups)

Procedure

1. Drain orange sections, reserving juice.

2. Dissolve gelatin and salt in boiling water.

3. Measure crushed ice. Add reserved orange juice and just enough water to cover ice. Add to gelatin, stirring constantly until ice is melted. Add orange peel.

4. When gelatin is slightly thickened, fold in oranges, bananas, and coconut. Pour into individual molds; chill until firm.

5. Unmold; serve with whipped cream or Creamy Vanilla Sauce. (See recipe, page 212.)

IN-THE-PINK PINEAPPLE PUNCH

Yield: 50 5-ounce portions

Ingredients

PINEAPPLE TIDBITS	1 No. 10 can
GELATIN, STRAWBERRY FLAVOR	1-1/2 pounds
MINIATURE MARSHMALLOWS	6-1/4 ounces
WATER, boiling	2 quarts
PINEAPPLE SYRUP RESERVED FROM	1 No. 10 can
WATER, cold	2 cups
ORANGE JUICE CONCENTRATE, thawed	1 cup
BANANA SLICES	2 pounds, 12 ounces
WHIPPED TOPPING	as needed

Procedure

1. Drain pineapple, reserving syrup.
2. Dissolve gelatin and marshmallows in boiling water. Add reserved pineapple syrup, cold water, and orange juice concentrate.
3. Chill until mixture mounds on a spoon.
4. Fold in drained pineapple and bananas.
5. Turn into punch cups; chill until firm. Serve with whipped topping.

Whipped Gelatin Desserts

PEAR-APPLESAUCE WHIP

Yield: 48 portions

Ingredients

GELATINE, UNFLAVORED	4 ounces
SUGAR	3 cups
PEAR SYRUP, DRAINED FROM PEARS	2 quarts
LEMON JUICE	1/2 cup
APPLESAUCE	1 quart
WHIPPED TOPPING	2 quarts
BARTLETT PEARS, CANNED (DESSERT CHUNK PACK), drained	2 quarts
CUSTARD SAUCE	1-1/2 quarts

Procedure

1. Mix gelatine and sugar in saucepan. Stir in pear syrup.
2. Place over low heat, stir until sugar and gelatine are completely dissolved.
3. Add lemon juice and applesauce.
4. Chill until mixture begins to thicken. Beat until light and fluffy.
5. Fold in whipped topping and pear chunks.
6. Turn into individual molds or shallow pans. Chill until firm.
7. Unmold or cut into squares. Serve with custard sauce.

APPLESAUCE PUMPKIN CHIFFON PUDDING

Yield: 48 portions

Ingredients

GELATINE, UNFLAVORED	3/4 cup
APPLE JUICE	3 cups
APPLE SAUCE, CANNED	1 No. 10 can
PUMPKIN, CANNED	1-1/2 quarts
SOUR CREAM	3 cups
SALT	1-1/2 teaspoons
SUGAR, GRANULATED	1-1/2 cups
CINNAMON, GROUND	1 tablespoon
CLOVES, GROUND	1-1/2 teaspoons
NUTMEG, GROUND	1-1/2 teaspoons
MILK, EVAPORATED, chilled	1-1/2 quarts
GINGERSNAP CRUMBS	3 pounds
BUTTER *OR* MARGARINE, melted	1 pound

Procedure

1. Soften gelatine in apple juice. Place over low heat; stir until gelatine is dissolved.

2. Combine apple sauce, pumpkin, sour cream, salt, sugar, and spices. Add gelatine; mix thoroughly.

3. Chill until thick and syrupy.

4. Chill evaporated milk until crystals form around edge. Beat until it holds soft peaks.

5. Fold whipped milk into apple sauce mixture.

6. Blend gingersnap crumbs with melted butter stirring to thoroughly coat crumbs.

7. Turn 1 quart crumbs into each of two 12-inch by 20-inch by 2-1/2-inch pans. Press to line bottoms of pans evenly.

8. Put apple sauce mixture into pans, dividing equally. Sprinkle with remaining crumbs.

9. Chill until firm. Serve with whipped cream or whipped topping, if desired.

STRAWBERRY WHIP ALMONDINE

Yield: 48 portions

Ingredients

GELATIN, STRAWBERRY FLAVOR	1-1/2 pounds
WATER, boiling	2 quarts
WATER, cold	2 quarts
ALMOND CUSTARD SAUCE (*see recipe,*	2 quarts
below) *OR* WHIPPED CREAM, sweetened	1-1/2 to 2 quarts
ALMONDS, sliced, natural	1-1/3 cups

Procedure

1. Dissolve gelatin in boiling water in mixer bowl. Add cold water. Chill until consistency of heavy syrup or unbeaten egg white.

2. Whip at medium speed, using balloon whip, 10 to 12 minutes or until mixture is fluffy and thick and has doubled in bulk.

3. Turn into two 12-inch by 20-inch by 2-inch pans; chill until firm. Or, turn into parfait glasses; place on trays; chill until firm.

4. To serve, spoon whip from pans into dessert dishes. Top with 1-1/2 ounces custard sauce; sprinkle with almonds. Or, top parfaits with whipped cream; garnish with almonds.

ALMOND CUSTARD SAUCE

Yield: 2-1/4 quarts

Ingredients

MILK	2 quarts
SUGAR	1 cup
CORNSTARCH	1/4 cup
SALT	1/2 teaspoon
EGGS, WHOLE *OR*	5
EGG YOLKS	9 (3/4 cup)
ALMOND EXTRACT	1/4 teaspoon

Procedure

1. Scald milk in double boiler or steam jacketed kettle or heavy saucepan over low heat.

2. Mix sugar, cornstarch, and salt; stir into hot milk. Cook, stirring frequently, 5 to 7 minutes. Remove from heat.

3. Beat eggs lightly. Gradually blend hot mixture with eggs, stirring constantly.

4. Add almond extract. Chill thoroughly.

APPLE CHARLOTTE

Yield: 40 portions

Ingredients

GELATINE, UNFLAVORED	1 ounce
WATER, cold	1 cup
WATER, boiling	1 cup
SUGAR	1-1/2 pounds
LEMON JUICE	6 tablespoons
APPLE SAUCE, CANNED	1 quart
EGG WHITES	8 (1 cup)

Procedure

1. Soak gelatine in cold water 10 minutes.

2. Add boiling water; stir until gelatine is dissolved. Add sugar, lemon juice, and apple sauce.

3. Chill until mixture begins to thicken.

4. Beat egg whites for 2 minutes at high speed; add gelatine and apple sauce mixture and continue beating 4 or 5 minutes until mixture is light and even in texture. (Overbeating causes mixture to be coarse-grained.)

5. Pour into shallow pans; chill until set. Cut into squares.

6. Serve with a lemon custard sauce or with sweetened, fresh berries.

PINEAPPLE FOAM

Yield: 25 portions

Ingredients

GELATINE, UNFLAVORED	3 tablespoons
ORANGE JUICE	2 cups
PINEAPPLE JUICE	1-1/2 quarts
PINEAPPLE TIDBITS, well drained	3 cups
MARASCHINO CHERRIES, drained, halved	1 cup
RASPBERRY SYRUP	1 quart

Procedure

1. Soak gelatine in orange juice 10 minutes. Heat, stirring, over low heat until gelatine is dissolved.

2. Stir pineapple juice slowly into gelatine mixture. Chill until consistency of egg white.

3. Beat on mixer until frothy and stiff enough to hold shape.

4. Fold in drained pineapple and maraschino cherries.

5. Pour into pans or into individual parfait or sherbet dishes. Chill until firm.

6. Serve with raspberry syrup.

FRESH ORANGE DESSERT

Yield: 24 portions

Ingredients

GELATINE, UNFLAVORED	1 ounce
WATER, cold	1 cup
WATER, hot	1 quart
SUGAR	8 ounces
SALT	1/2 teaspoon
ORANGE JUICE	2 cups
LEMON JUICE	1/4 cup
ORANGE SECTIONS	3 cups

Procedure

1. Soften gelatine in cold water. Dissolve in hot water; add sugar and salt; stir until dissolved. Add orange and lemon juices.

2. Divide 1 quart of the gelatine mixture into 24 individual molds allowing about 3 tablespoons per mold. Chill until slightly thickened. Arrange orange sections on top of gelatine.

3. Chill remaining gelatine until consistency of egg whites. Whip until light and fluffy and double in bulk; spoon over oranges.

4. Chill until firm. Unmold; serve with custard sauce.

LEMON SNOW

Yield: 75 3/4 cup molds or
3 pans 18 inches by 12 inches by 2-1/2-inches

Ingredients

GELATINE, UNFLAVORED	2 ounces
WATER, cold	3 cups
WATER, boiling	1-1/2 quarts
SUGAR	1-1/2 cups
SALT	1/8 teaspoon
FROZEN LEMON JUICE CONCENTRATE*	24 ounces (3 cups)
EGG WHITES (room temperature)	4
ICE WATER	2 cups
NONFAT DRY MILK	1/2 pound

Procedure

1. Soften gelatine in the cold water. Dissolve in the boiling water. Cool slightly.

2. Add sugar, salt, and lemon juice concentrate; stir until sugar is dissolved. Chill until slightly thickened.

3. Place egg whites and cold water in a 20-quart mixer bowl. Add nonfat dry milk. Beat at high speed until stiff.

4. Add gelatine mixture. Continue beating until light and fluffy.

5. Turn into molds or pans. Chill until firm.

6. Unmold or cut into squares. Serve with custard sauce, or with fresh or frozen strawberry or raspberry sauce.

*Or use half lemon and half lime or orange juice.

LEMON SNOW WITH CUSTARD SAUCE

Yield: 8 pans (12 inches by 18 inches by 2-1/2-inches), 320 portions

Ingredients

GELATINE, UNFLAVORED	1-1/3 cups
WATER, cold	1-1/4 quarts
WATER, boiling	1-1/4 gallons
SUGAR	1-1/4 gallons
LEMON JUICE, FRESH, strained	1-1/4 quarts
EGG WHITES	60 (2 quarts)
VANILLA CUSTARD SAUCE (*see recipe, below*)	3-1/2 gallons

Procedure

1. Soften gelatine in cold water.
2. Dissolve in boiling water. Add sugar; stir until dissolved.
3. Add lemon juice. Chill until thick and syrupy (when a spoon drawn through mixture leaves a definite trace).
4. Beat egg whites until stiff but not dry. Add gelatine mixture; continue to beat until mixture holds its shape.
5. Turn into pans; chill until firm. Serve with custard sauce.

VANILLA CUSTARD SAUCE

Yield: 3-1/2 gallons

Ingredients

MILK	2-1/2 gallons
SUGAR	1-3/4 quarts
CORNSTARCH	2 cups
SALT	1 tablespoon
EGG YOLKS, beaten	60 (1-1/4 quarts)
VANILLA	1/2 cup

Procedure

1. Heat milk to boiling point.
2. Combine sugar, cornstarch, and salt, mix thoroughly. Add to hot milk, stirring constantly.
3. Cook, stirring, until thickened.
4. Add about a quart of the hot mixture to beaten egg yolks; blend. Return to hot mixture gradually, stirring constantly. Continue to cook a few minutes longer until the desired consistency.
5. Remove from heat; add vanilla. Cool.

LIME GINGER JELLY

Yield: 24 portions

Ingredients

GELATIN, LIME FLAVOR	13 ounces
WATER, boiling	1 quart
GINGERALE	1 quart
CREAM, HEAVY	1 cup
APRICOTS, SLICED	1 No. 303 can

Procedure

1. Dissolve gelatin in boiling water. Cool slightly; add gingerale.

2. Chill until slightly thickened. Whip in mixer until light and doubled in bulk.

3. Whip cream until thick and shiny; fold into gelatin mixture. Turn into individual molds or shallow pan. Chill until set.

4. Unmold or cut into squares. Serve with a spoonful of sliced apricots.

California Apricot Advisory Board/ National Cherry Growers and Industries Foundation

Quick and Easy—Ready-Made Tart Shells, Prepared Pudding, and Colorful Canned Fruit

MELON FLUFF COOLER

Yield: 50 portions

Ingredients

GELATIN, LEMON FLAVOR	1-1/2 pounds
WATER, hot	2 quarts
WATER, cold	1-1/2 quarts
COINTREAU OR OTHER ORANGE FLAVORED LIQUEUR*	2 cups
MELON BALLS, drained	2 quarts

Procedure

1. Dissolve gelatin in hot water. Add cold water and liqueur. Chill until slightly thickened.

2. Measure 2-2/3 quarts or two-thirds of the mixture; add melon balls. Portion into serving dishes. Chill until set but not firm.

3. Whip remaining gelatin mixture until fluffy and thick, about double in volume. Ladle over set gelatin. Chill until firm.

4. Garnish with additional melon balls and sprigs of mint, if desired.
Or orange juice.

LIME WHIP

Yield: 48 1/2-cup portions

Ingredients

GELATINE, UNFLAVORED	1 ounce
SUGAR	3 cups
SALT	1 teaspoon
WATER	3 cups
LIME JUICE	1 cup
LIME PEEL, grated	2 tablespoons
WATER	2 cups
EGG WHITES	8 (1 cup)

Procedure

1. Mix gelatine, sugar, and salt in saucepan. Add first amount of water, heat, stirring until gelatine and sugar are dissolved.

2. Pour into mixer bowl. Add lime juice, grated peel, and remaining water. Chill to unbeaten egg white consistency.

3. Add the egg whites. Beat until mixture holds its shape. Pile into individual dessert dishes or into large shallow pan 18 inches by 12 inches by 2 inches. Chill until firm.

Cream, Bavarian, and Similar Molded Desserts

CUSTARD CREME

Yield: 50 1/2-cup portions

Ingredients	
GELATINE, UNFLAVORED	7 tablespoons
CORNSTARCH	1/4 cup
SUGAR	2 cups
SALT	2 teaspoons
MILK, cold	1-1/2 quarts
MILK, scalded	3-3/4 quarts
EGGS, lightly beaten	25 (2-1/2 pounds)
VANILLA	3 tablespoons
CREAM, whipped *OR*	
WHIPPED TOPPING	1 quart
STRAWBERRIES, sliced,	
sweetened	1-3/4 quarts

Procedure

1. Combine gelatine, cornstarch, sugar, and salt. Gradually stir in cold milk.

2. Stir mixture vigorously into scalded milk. Place over low heat or hot water; stir constantly until gelatine is dissolved and cornstarch is cooked.

3. Blend about a quart of the hot mixture into the beaten eggs. Return to the remaining hot mixture, stirring vigorously. Cook the custard mixture over low heat or hot water, stirring constantly, 5 minutes or until mixture coats a metal spoon.

4. Remove from heat; add vanilla. Pour into individual molds or custard cups allowing 4 ounces (1/2 cup) per portion. Chill until set. Unmold; garnish with whipped cream or topping and strawberries.

229

SPANISH CREAM

Yield: 24 2/3-cup portions

Ingredients

GELATINE, UNFLAVORED	1 ounce
SUGAR	1/2 cup
SALT	1/2 teaspoon
EGG YOLKS	10
MILK *OR* HALF AND HALF	2 quarts
VANILLA	5 teaspoons
EGG WHITES	10
SUGAR	1 cup

Procedure

1. Combine gelatine, first amount of sugar, and salt in saucepan.

2. Beat egg yolks with one-half of the milk (or half and half). Add to gelatine mixture.

3. Place over low heat, stirring constantly, until gelatine is dissolved. Remove from heat. Add remaining milk and vanilla. Chill until mixture mounds slightly when dropped from a spoon.

4. Beat egg whites until foamy throughout; add sugar gradually; continue beating until meringue is very stiff.

5. Fold into gelatine mixture. Pour into individual molds. Chill until set.

6. Unmold. Serve with chocolate sauce or crushed, sweetened raspberries.

STRAWBERRY BAVARIAN CREAM

Yield: 50 portions, No. 12 scoop

Ingredients

GELATINE, UNFLAVORED	6 tablespoons
WATER, cold	3 cups
LEMON JUICE	1 cup
SUGAR	1 quart
SALT	1 teaspoon
WATER, boiling	3 cups
STRAWBERRIES, FRESH OR FROZEN	2 quarts
CREAM, HEAVY	1-1/2 quarts

Procedure

1. Soften gelatine in cold water.

2. Add lemon juice, sugar, salt, and softened gelatine to boiling water. Stir until dissolved. Chill until slightly thickened.

3. If fresh strawberries are used, clean, hull, and crush slightly. Add strawberries to the slightly thickened gelatine.

4. Whip cream until thick and shiny; fold into gelatine mixture. Chill until firm.

5. Serve in sherbet dishes; garnish with additional whipped cream and a fresh whole strawberry, if desired.

Cling Peach Advisory Board

Peach-Orange Whip, Mint Leaf Garnish

GRAPE JUICE BAVARIAN

Yield: 64 portions

Ingredients

GELATIN, LEMON FLAVOR	1-1/2 pounds
SUGAR	2 cups
WATER, hot	2 quarts
GRAPE JUICE, cold	2 quarts
WHIPPED TOPPING MIX	1 12-1/4-ounce envelope
WATER, ice-cold	3-3/4 cups

Procedure

1. Dissolve gelatin and sugar in hot water. Add grape juice. Chill until slightly thickened.
2. Prepare topping mix with water according to package directions.
3. Blend in slightly thickened gelatin.
4. Spoon into serving dishes. Chill until firm.

LEMON PUDDING DELUXE

Yield: 25 portions

Ingredients

GELATIN, LEMON FLAVOR	1-1/4 cups
SALT	1/2 teaspoon
SUGAR	1 cup
WATER, BOILING	1-1/4 quarts
LEMON JUICE	2/3 cup
CREAM, HEAVY	1-1/4 cups

Procedure

1. Dissolve the gelatin, salt, and sugar in boiling water.
2. Add lemon juice; chill until slightly thickened.
3. Whip cream until thick and shiny but not stiff; fold into gelatin mixture.
4. Turn into molds; chill until firm.
5. Unmold; serve with crushed strawberries or raspberries or with custard sauce.

HAZELNUT BAVARIAN CREAM

Yield: 24 portions

Ingredients

GELATINE	3 tablespoons
WATER, cold	6 tablespoons
MILK, scalded	1-1/2 cups
SUGAR, GRANULATED	3/4 cup
EGG YOLKS, beaten	12 (1 cup)
SALT	1/4 teaspoon
HAZELNUTS, ground	2-1/4 cups
VANILLA	1 tablespoon
CREAM, HEAVY	1 quart

Procedure

1. Soak gelatine in cold water.

2. Combine milk, sugar, egg yolks, and salt. Cook stirring over low heat until mixture begins to thicken.

3. Add softened gelatine, stir until dissolved.

4. Chill until slightly thickened; add hazelnuts and vanilla.

5. Whip cream; fold into gelatine mixture.

6. Pour into individual molds or into a 12-inch by 18-inch pan; chill until firm.

7. Serve with raspberry or loganberry syrup.

PINK STRAWBERRY MOUSSE

Yield: 10 to 12 portions

Ingredients

STRAWBERRIES, FROZEN, WHOLE, thawed, well drained	1 quart
SUGAR	1/2 cup
MARASCHINO LIQUEUR	1/2 cup
GELATINE, UNFLAVORED	2 tablespoons
WATER, cold	1/2 cup
WATER, boiling	1/2 cup
CREAM, HEAVY	2 cups

Procedure

1. Reserve several strawberries for garnish. Press remaining berries through fine sieve. Add sugar and liqueur; stir to dissolve sugar. Chill.

2. Soften gelatine in cold water. Add boiling water, stirring to dissolve. Cool.

3. Combine gelatine and chilled strawberry mixture. Beat until fluffy and slightly thickened.

4. Whip cream. Fold into gelatine. Turn into a 2-quart mold. Chill until firm.

5. Unmold onto chilled platter. Garnish with reserved whole berries.

COCOA PUDDING MOLD

Yield: 32 portions

Ingredients

GELATINE, UNFLAVORED	6 tablespoons
MILK, cold	2 cups
COCOA	1-3/4 cups (6 ounces)
SUGAR	3 cups
SALT	1/2 teaspoon
MILK	2-3/4 quarts
CREAM, LIGHT	2 cups
VANILLA	1 tablespoon

Procedure

1. Soften gelatine in cold milk.

2. Combine cocoa, sugar, salt, milk, and light cream. Heat over hot water until blended.

3. Add softened gelatine; stir until dissolved. Remove mixture from hot water.

4. Add vanilla; blend. Chill, stirring occasionally, until slightly thickened.

5. Turn into individual molds or sherbet dishes. Chill until firm.

6. Serve plain, or with cream or custard sauce.

CHOCOLATE MARSHMALLOW CREAM

Yield: 48 1/2-cup portions

Ingredients

GELATINE, UNFLAVORED	1-1/2 ounces
SUGAR	2 cups
MILK	1-1/2 quarts
CHOCOLATE, UNSWEETENED	1/2 pound
LEMON JUICE	1 tablespoon
VANILLA	2 tablespoons
EGG WHITES	8 (1 cup)
SALT	1/2 teaspoon
SUGAR	1/2 cup
CREAM, HEAVY	2 cups
MARSHMALLOWS, cut in small pieces	1/2 pound

Procedure

1. Combine gelatine and first amount of sugar in top of double boiler. Add milk and chocolate. Stir over simmering water until chocolate is melted. Remove from heat.

2. Add lemon juice and vanilla. Beat until smooth. Chill to unbeaten egg white consistency, stirring frequently.

3. Beat egg whites and salt until foamy. Beat in remaining sugar, 1 tablespoon at a time; beat until stiff peaks form.

4. Fold into chocolate mixture just until blended.

5. Whip cream until stiff. Fold cream and marshmallows into chocolate mixture, blending gently.

6. Turn into molds. Chill until firm. Unmold; serve garnished with additional whipped cream, if desired.

MARRON CHARLOTTE

Yield: 24 portions

Ingredients

GELATINE, UNFLAVORED	1-1/2 ounces
WATER, cold	3/4 cup
WATER, boiling	3/4 cup
EGG YOLKS	12 (1 cup)
SHERRY WINE	3 cups
CREAM, HEAVY, whipped	2 quarts
MARRONS, cut fine	3 cups

Procedure

1. Soak gelatine in cold water; dissolve in boiling water.
2. Beat yolks until thick and lemon-colored; beat in wine.
3. Add dissolved gelatine; mix thoroughly. Chill until slightly thickened.
4. Fold in whipped cream and marrons. Turn into molds.
5. Chill until firm. Serve with additional sweetened whipped cream. Garnish with maraschino cherry and a small green leaf or two, as desired.

Florida Department of Citrus

Tangy Grapefruit Sections Circle Chilled Creme

MAPLE CREAM

Yield: 24 portions

Ingredients

GELATINE	1/4 cup
MILK, cold	1 cup
MILK, scalded	2-1/4 quarts
EGG YOLKS, beaten	12 (1 cup)
MAPLE SYRUP	2-2/3 cups
VANILLA	1 tablespoon
EGG WHITES	12 (1-1/2 cups)
SALT	1 teaspoon

Procedure

1. Soak gelatine in cold milk. Add to scalded milk; stir until dissolved.

2. Pour over the beaten yolks, stirring constantly. Return to low heat and cook until mixture begins to thicken.

3. Remove from heat. Slowly add maple syrup and vanilla.

4. Beat egg whites with salt until stiff but not dry. Fold into gelatine mixture.

5. Pour into individual molds or into 12-inch by 18-inch pudding pan. Chill until firm.

6. Serve with cream or custard sauce.

CHARLOTTE RUSSE

Yield: 48 portions

Ingredients

GELATINE, UNFLAVORED	2 ounces
WATER, cold	3 cups
WATER, boiling	3 cups
SUGAR	1-1/2 pounds
SALT	1 teaspoon
LEMON JUICE FROM	3 lemons
VANILLA	4 teaspoons
MARASCHINO CHERRY RINGS	1/2 cup
CREAM 20%	3 cups
CREAM, HEAVY	1-1/2 quarts
LADY FINGERS	12 dozen
MARASCHINO CHERRY RINGS	48

Procedure

1. Soak gelatine in cold water 5 minutes. Add boiling water, stirring until gelatine is completely dissolved.

2. Add sugar, salt, lemon juice, and vanilla. Chill in an ice and water bath until slightly thickened.

3. Whip until light and fluffy; fold in first amount of cherry rings and 20% cream.

4. Whip cream. Fold half of it into gelatine mixture, reserve half for garnish.

5. Fill sherbet dishes. Garnish each portion with 3 lady fingers, 1/2 ounce of whipped cream, and one cherry ring.

GRAHAM APRICOT CREAM TORTE

Yield: 24 portions

Ingredients

APRICOT HALVES	1 No. 10 can
GELATINE, UNFLAVORED	1-1/2 ounces
SUGAR	1 cup
WHIPPED TOPPING MIX	8-1/2 ounces
MILK	2 cups
VANILLA	2 teaspoons
GRAHAM CRACKERS	48 squares
WHIPPED TOPPING, prepared	as needed
MARASCHINO CHERRIES	24

Procedure

1. Drain apricots, reserving syrup.

2. Sprinkle gelatine over about 1 cup of the syrup to soften; then stir over hot water until completely dissolved.

3. Mash apricot halves; combine with remaining syrup, gelatine mixture, and sugar. Refrigerate until mixture mounds when dropped from spoon.

4. Beat whipped topping mix with milk and vanilla according to package directions. Fold into apricot mixture.

5. Spread about a third of the mixture into a 12-inch by 20-inch pan. Top with 24 graham cracker squares. Top with half of remaining apricot mixture, remaining crackers, then remaining apricot mixture.

6. Refrigerate overnight, or until set.

7. Cut into portions. Garnish with prepared whipped topping and cherries.

STRAWBERRY MARBLE CREAM

Yield: 24 portions

Ingredients

GELATIN, LEMON FLAVOR	2 cups
WATER, hot	1-1/2 quarts
FROZEN STRAWBERRIES, SLICED, thawed	5 cups
GELATINE, UNFLAVORED	1/4 cup
CREAM, HEAVY	1 quart
WALNUTS, chopped	1 cup

Procedure

1. Dissolve lemon gelatin in hot water. Chill until slightly thickened.

2. Drain strawberries; reserve juice. Soften unflavored gelatine in 1 cup of the juice. Dissolve over hot water. Add strawberries and remaining strawberry juice. Chill until slightly thickened.

3. Whip cream until thick; continue beating while gradually adding slightly thickened lemon gelatin mixture.

4. Sprinkle walnuts in bottom of a 12-inch by 18-inch shallow pan. Top with whipped cream mixture. Add strawberry mixture; cut through with a spatula to give a marbled effect. Chill until firm.

ORANGE-DATE WHIP

Yield: 48 portions

Ingredients

GELATINE, UNFLAVORED	6 tablespoons
ORANGE JUICE	3-1/4 quarts
SUGAR, GRANULATED	2 cups
SALT	1/2 teaspoon
DATES, granules or pieces	1-1/2 quarts
BREAD CUBES, SOFT, 1/2-inch	3 quarts (1 pound)
NONFAT DRY MILK	3 cups (12 ounces)
ORANGE JUICE	3 cups
SUGAR, GRANULATED	1 cup
VANILLA EXTRACT	1-1/2 teaspoons
ALMOND EXTRACT	2 teaspoons

Procedure

1. Chill mixing bowl and beater thoroughly.

2. Soak gelatine in 3 cups of the orange juice.

3. Combine 2-1/2 quarts orange juice with sugar and salt in a one-gallon saucepan. Boil about 5 minutes. Add dates and soft bread cubes.

4. Combine hot mixture with soaked gelatine. Chill until slightly thickened.

5. Combine nonfat dry milk and remaining orange juice in chilled bowl. Beat at high speed until stiff. Beat in remaining sugar, vanilla, and almond extracts. (Entire beating takes about 15 minutes.)

6. Fold the whipped milk into gelatine mixture. Pour into two 10-inch by 18-inch by 2-inch pans. Chill until firm.

WHITE MOUNTAIN

Yield: 14 portions

Ingredients

GELATINE, UNFLAVORED	3 tablespoons
WATER, cold	3/4 cup
EGGS	5
SALT	1/8 teaspoon
SUGAR	1 cup
CREAM, HEAVY*	1 quart
KAHLUA	1 cup

Procedure

1. Soften gelatine in cold water. Dissolve over hot water.
2. Combine eggs and salt. Beat until light and frothy. Add sugar; continue to beat until thick and lemon-colored.
3. Beat gelatine into egg mixture.
4. Whip cream until stiff.
5. Fold egg mixture and Kahlua into cream until ingredients are thoroughly blended.
6. Fill a 2-1/2-quart mold or bowl with dessert mixture. Pour remainder into a 10-ounce custard cup or bowl.
7. Chill until firmly set.
8. Unmold large mold onto serving tray. Unmold custard cup; place on top of large mold.
9. Decorate with additional whipped cream or whipped topping, frosted cookies, and shaved chocolate, as desired.

Or 2 quarts prepared whipped topping.

MARASCHINO JEWEL CAKE

Yield: 4 cakes (48 portions)

Ingredients

GRAHAM CRACKER CRUMBS	1 pound
SUGAR	1-1/3 cups
BUTTER *OR* MARGARINE, melted	1 pound
GELATIN, CHERRY FLAVOR	12 ounces
WATER, hot	1 quart
MARASCHINO CHERRY SYRUP	2 cups
GELATIN, BLACK CHERRY OR RASPBERRY FLAVOR	12 ounces
WATER, hot	1-1/2 quarts
GELATIN, LEMON FLAVOR	12 ounces
SUGAR	1 cup
WATER, hot	1-1/2 quarts
PINEAPPLE, CANNED, CRUSHED	2 pounds
LEMON JUICE	3/4 cup
SALT	1/2 teaspoon
MARASCHINO CHERRIES, chopped, drained	3 cups
CREAM, HEAVY*	1-1/2 quarts

Procedure

1. Mix crumbs, first amount of sugar, and butter. Press on bottom and halfway up sides of four 9-inch spring-form pans.

2. Dissolve cherry gelatin in first amount of hot water. Add maraschino cherry syrup. Pour into shallow pan; chill until firm.

3. Dissolve black cherry or black raspberry gelatin in next amount of hot water. Pour into shallow pan; chill until firm.

4. Dissolve lemon gelatin and remaining sugar in remaining hot water. Add pineapple, lemon juice, and salt. Chill until slightly thickened. Beat until fluffy. Add cherries.

5. Whip cream; fold into pineapple mixture.

6. Cut cherry and black cherry or raspberry gelatin into 1/2-inch cubes. Fold into cream mixture.

7. Turn into crumb-lined pans. Chill until firm. Garnish with additional cherries, if desired.

Or, 3 quarts prepared whipped topping.

Parfait Sparkles with Blackberry Gelatin Cubes

SWEDISH CREAM

Yield: 24 portions

Ingredients

SOUR CREAM	1-1/2 quarts
SUGAR	3 cups
GELATINE, UNFLAVORED	3 tablespoons
CREAM, HEAVY	1-1/2 quarts
VANILLA	1 tablespoon

Procedure

1. Allow sour cream to warm to room temperature.

2. Mix sugar, gelatine, and heavy cream in a saucepan. Heat, stirring, over low heat until gelatine has lost granular appearance and is completely dissolved.

3. Cool until just slightly thickened and approximately room temperature.

4. Carefully stir sour cream until smooth. Blend sour cream and vanilla into gelatine mixture until ingredients are well blended.

5. Turn into lightly oiled, individual molds. Chill until firm.

6. To unmold, gently slip knife around edge of mold; turn into large sherbet dish. Serve with a pie filling fruit sauce, crushed sweetened berries, or other appropriate sauce, as desired.

ROMAN PARFAIT

Yield: 30 portions

Ingredients

GELATIN, LIME FLAVOR	12 ounces
WATER, boiling	1 quart
INSTANT PUDDING MIX, VANILLA FLAVOR	13 ounces
LIQUID INSTANT MILK	2 quarts
ORANGE PEEL, grated	2 tablespoons
ORANGES, SEEDLESS, sliced or sectioned	10
WHIPPED TOPPING MIX	9 ounces (half package)
MARASCHINO CHERRIES	30

Procedure

1. Dissolve lime gelatin in boiling water. Chill until consistency of unbeaten egg whites.

2. Combine instant pudding powder and liquid instant milk; beat, using low speed on mixer, until thickened.

3. Fold gelatin into pudding. Add grated orange peel. Blend at low speed for 5 minutes, using wire whip of mixer.

4. Spoon pudding into parfait glasses, filling 3/4 full. Insert sections of oranges.

5. Prepare whip topping according to package directions. Spoon on top of parfaits.

6. Garnish with maraschino cherries. Chill.

CHILLED SOUFFLES

LOFTY, CHILLED SOUFFLES lend themselves to endless variation with exciting additions and imaginative flavorings. They inspire wonderful presentations and welcome the use of sauces, garnishes, and other flourishes. A dressed-up version can easily become the star attraction on a dessert cart or buffet.

Advisory Council for Jams, Jellies and Preserves

Apricot Jam Souffle and Apricot Ginger Sauce

APRICOT JAM SOUFFLE
(see picture, opposite)

Yield: 3 quarts

Ingredients

GELATINE, UNFLAVORED	3 tablespoons
SUGAR	3/4 cup
EGG YOLKS, beaten	6 (1/2 cup)
APRICOT PRESERVES	1-1/2 cups (15 ounces)
LEMON JUICE	1 cup
EGG WHITES	6 (3/4 cup)
SUGAR	3/4 cup
CREAM, HEAVY	1-1/2 cups

Procedure

1. Combine gelatine, sugar, egg yolks, preserves, and lemon juice. Stir over low heat until mixture just comes to a boil. Remove from heat. Chill until mixture mounds when dropped from a spoon.

2. Beat egg whites until foamy throughout; gradually beat in sugar until stiff and glossy. Fold into gelatine mixture.

3. Whip cream. Gently fold into mixture.

4. Make a 3-inch high foil collar around a 1-1/2-quart souffle dish. Pour in souffle; chill until firm.

5. To serve, remove collar; garnish as desired and serve with Apricot Ginger Sauce. See following recipe.

Garnish suggestions

1. Arrange a border of canned apricot slices on top.

2. Pipe a border of whipped cream or topping around top.

3. Press toasted coconut, toasted sliced almonds, or grated semi-sweet chocolate onto sides of souffle.

APRICOT GINGER SAUCE

Yield: 2-1/2 cups

Ingredients

APRICOT PRESERVES	2 cups
GRAND MARNIER, TRIPLE SEC, OR COINTREAU	1/2 cup
CRYSTALLIZED GINGER, chopped	2 tablespoons
LEMON JUICE	1 tablespoon

Procedure

1. Combine ingredients; chill until ready to serve.

MOCHA CHEESE SOUFFLE (DESSERT)

Yield: 2 6-portion souffles, or 3 4-portion souffles,
or 12 individual souffles.

Ingredients

GELATINE, UNFLAVORED	2 tablespoons
INSTANT COFFEE POWDER	1 tablespoon
SUGAR	1-1/2 cups
WATER, boiling	2-1/2 cups
COTTAGE CHEESE	3 cups
EGG YOLKS	4
VANILLA	2 tablespoons
CREAM, HEAVY, chilled	2 cups
SALT	1/4 teaspoon
EGG WHITES, warmed to room temperature	4
WHIPPED CREAM	to garnish
SHAVED CHOCOLATE	to garnish

Procedure

1. Tie a band of aluminum foil firmly around the souffle dishes to be used so that foil extends 2 inches above rim of dish. (Note: A 1-quart souffle dish holds 6 cups souffle mixture, makes service for six.)

2. Mix gelatine, coffee powder, and sugar. Add boiling water; stir until dry mixture is completely dissolved. Chill until syrupy.

3. Beat cheese, egg yolks, and vanilla until mixture is almost smooth and has a light lemony color. Do not underbeat.

4. Whip cream until thick and glossy, but not stiff.

5. Set bowl of slightly thickened gelatine mixture in a larger bowl of ice and water. Beat with a rotary beater 5 minutes or until light and fluffy and about double in volume.

6. Add the cheese mixture; beat thoroughly to blend. Gently fold in the whipped cream.

7. Add salt to egg whites. Beat until whites just begin to form peaks. Fold carefully into souffle mixture.

8. Pour into prepared souffle dishes. Chill in refrigerator overnight.

9. To serve, remove foil band. Decorate top with whipped cream and shaved chocolate. Serve with Velvety Chocolate Sauce. See following recipe.

VELVETY CHOCOLATE SAUCE

Yield: 1 quart

Ingredients

SEMI-SWEET CHOCOLATE PIECES	1 pound, 2 ounces
SUGAR, DARK BROWN	1 cup
WATER	2/3 cup
SOUR CREAM	2 cups
VANILLA	1 tablespoon
SALT	1/8 teaspoon

Procedure

1. Combine chocolate pieces, sugar, and water in heavy saucepan. Place over low heat. When chocolate pieces become soft, stir constantly until mixture is smooth.

2. Remove from heat. Add sour cream, vanilla, and salt; mix until thoroughly blended. Cool.

Note

Sauce may be stored in refrigerator. It will set upon standing. Beat gently with a spoon to restore original consistency before serving.

FROSTED DAIQUIRI SOUFFLE

Yield: 24 portions

Ingredients

EGG YOLKS	1-1/4 cups
SUGAR	1-1/2 cups
LIME JUICE, freshly squeezed	3/4 cup
LEMON JUICE, freshly squeezed	3/4 cup
LIME PEEL, grated	1 tablespoon
LEMON PEEL, grated	2 tablespoons
GREEN FOOD COLORING, optional	few drops
GELATINE, UNFLAVORED	3 tablespoons
RUM, LIGHT	6 ounces
EGG WHITES	2 cups
SUGAR	3/4 cup
CREAM, HEAVY*	3 cups
SUGAR	3/4 cup
CREAM, HEAVY*	1-1/2 cups
SUGAR	2 tablespoons
ALMONDS, sliced, toasted	2 cups
LIMES, THINLY SLICED	5

continued next page

FROSTED DAIQUIRI SOUFFLE, *cont'd.*

Procedure

1. Beat egg yolks until light and fluffy; add first amount of sugar gradually, beating until smooth.

2. Add fruit juices and grated peel: mix until well blended.

3. Cook, stirring, over low heat until thickened. Add green coloring, if desired.

4. Soften gelatine in rum; stir into hot mixture to dissolve. Cool thoroughly.

5. Beat egg whites to soft peak stage. Add next amount of sugar gradually, continuing to beat until stiff.

6. Whip first amount of cream with next amount of sugar until stiff.

7. Fold egg whites into gelatine mixture. Fold in whipped cream.

8. Portion into individual serving dishes, allowing approximately 3/4 cup per portion. Refrigerate.

9. At serving time, whip remaining cream and remaining sugar until stiff. Garnish portions with whipped cream, almonds, and a lime cartwheel twist.

Note

The flavor of souffle improves if it is made one day in advance and refrigerated. It also freezes well.

Or double the amount of prepared whipped topping.

LEMON SOUFFLE

Yield: 48 portions

Ingredients

GELATINE, UNFLAVORED	3/4 cup
WATER, cold	1 quart
SUGAR	1-1/2 quarts
EGG YOLKS, beaten	1 quart (2 pounds)
LEMON JUICE	3 quarts
LEMON PEEL, grated	1/4 cup
SALT	1 teaspoon
NUTMEG, GROUND	1 teaspoon
EGG WHITES	1-1/2 quarts (3 pounds)
SUGAR	1-1/2 quarts
CREAM, HEAVY*	1-1/2 quarts
SESAME SEEDS, toasted	1 cup

Procedure

1. Soften gelatine in cold water in top part of double boiler.
2. Add first amount of sugar, egg yolks, lemon juice, lemon peel, salt, and nutmeg; mix well.
3. Cook over hot, not boiling, water until mixture coats a metal spoon.
4. Chill until slightly thickened, stirring occasionally.
5. Beat egg whites until foamy throughout. Add remaining sugar gradually, continuing to beat until meringue forms stiff glossy peaks.
6. Whip cream.
7. Fold meringue and whipped cream into gelatine mixture, combining carefully until well blended.
8. Spoon mixture into individual souffle dishes fitted with buttered foil collars. Sprinkle with toasted sesame seeds.
9. Chill until firm. Remove foil. Serve without unmolding in the souffle dishes.

Note

To prepare collars, cut strips of foil 3 inches wide and long enough to fit around souffle dishes and overlap slightly. Fold in half lengthwise; butter one side and fit closely around top of dishes, letting top of foil extend about 1 inch above rim of dish. Overlap ends, fastening securely.

*Or 3 quarts prepared whipped topping.

MILE HIGH PINEAPPLE SOUFFLE

Yield: 10 portions

Ingredients

PINEAPPLE, CRUSHED (undrained)	2-1/2 cups
GELATINE, UNFLAVORED	2 tablespoons
EGG YOLKS	4
SUGAR	1/4 cup
SALT	1 teaspoon
VANILLA	1 teaspoon
ALMOND EXTRACT	1/2 teaspoon
LEMON JUICE	2 tablespoons
CREAM, HEAVY	1 cup
EGG WHITES	4
SUGAR	2 tablespoons

Procedure

1. Drain pineapple. Sprinkle gelatine over pineapple syrup; dissolve over hot water.

2. Beat egg yolks, first amount of sugar, salt, and flavoring extracts together until thick and lemon-colored. Beat in gelatine mixture.

3. Add drained pineapple and lemon juice. Chill until slightly thickened.

4. Whip cream.

5. Beat egg whites until foamy; gradually add remaining sugar, continuing to beat until soft peaks form. Fold in pineapple mixture. Fold in cream.

6. Turn into 6-inch (1 quart) souffle dish with 3-inch collar.* Chill until firm, at least 3 hours.

7. Remove collar. Garnish with additional pineapple, fresh mint leaves, and cherries, if desired.

*Tie or tape a double strip of aluminum foil securely around dish, allowing collar to extend 3 inches above edge of dish.

Sunkist Growers

Grapefruit Charlotte Russe

COFFEE SOUFFLE

Yield: 48 4-ounce portions

Ingredients

COFFEE	1-3/4 quarts
MILK	1-3/4 quarts
EGG YOLKS	1-1/8 cups
SUGAR	1 pound, 2 ounces
SALT	1-1/2 teaspoons
GELATINE, UNFLAVORED	2-1/4 ounces
WATER, cold	1-1/2 cups
EGG WHITES	2 cups
SUGAR	12 ounces
VANILLA	1 tablespoon
WHIPPED CREAM	1-1/2 quarts
WHIPPED CREAM (for garnish)	1 pound, 8 ounces

Procedure

1. Combine coffee and milk in double boiler; heat to scalding.

2. Beat egg yolks well; mix in a small amount of hot mixture. Add yolks to rest of hot mixture, mixing in quickly. Remove from heat.

3. Stir in first amount of sugar and salt.

4. Soften gelatine in cold water. Add to hot mixture; stir until gelatine dissolves. Chill overnight.

5. Beat egg whites with remaining sugar until very stiff. Add vanilla. Fold in whipped cream.

6. Stir gelatine mixture until smooth and free from lumps. Fold into cream and egg whites.

7. Dish only as needed into sherbet or other dessert dishes. Garnish each portion with 1/2 ounce of whipped cream.

CHOCOLATE VELVET SOUFFLE

Yield: 40 portions

Ingredients

HOT COCOA MIX	24 ounces
GELATINE, UNFLAVORED	1-1/2 ounces
SALT	2 teaspoons
WATER	3 cups
EGG YOLKS, slightly beaten	12 (1 cup)
VANILLA	2 teaspoons
MARSHMALLOW CREAM	1 quart
EGG WHITES	12 (1-1/2 cups)

Procedure

1. Combine cocoa mix, gelatine, and salt in top of double boiler.

2. Add water, egg yolks, and vanilla; blend. Cook, stirring, over hot water until mixture is slightly thickened and gelatine is dissolved.

3. Stir in marshmallow cream, blending thoroughly. Chill until mixture mounds when spooned.

4. Beat egg whites to moist peaks; fold into chocolate mixture.

5. Turn into individual souffle dishes or a 12-inch by 20-inch by 2-inch pan. Chill until firm.

6. Serve portions garnished with whipped cream and chopped nuts, if desired.

CHILLED CHERRY SOUFFLE

Yield: 10 to 12 portions

Ingredients

MARASCHINO CHERRIES, chopped	2/3 cup (28 cherries)
KIRSCH	1/2 cup
GELATINE, UNFLAVORED	2 tablespoons
SUGAR	2/3 cup
SALT	1/4 teaspoon
EGG YOLKS	8 (2/3 cup)
MILK	1 cup
WATER	1/2 cup
CREAM, HEAVY	2 cups
EGG WHITES	8 (1 cup)
SUGAR	1/2 cup

Procedure

1. Blend cherries with Kirsch in electric blender or food mill. Set aside.

2. Mix gelatine, first amount of sugar, and salt in top of double boiler. Beat in egg yolks until light. Gradually stir in milk and water.

3. Cook, stirring, over hot water until slightly thickened and gelatine dissolves.

4. Add cherry mixture. Chill until slightly thickened.

5. Whip cream.

6. Beat egg whites until foamy. Gradually add remaining sugar, beating until stiff but not dry. Fold into gelatine mixture. Fold in whipped cream.

7. Turn into a 1-1/2-quart souffle dish with a 3-inch collar. Chill until firm. Garnish with additional whipped cream and maraschino cherries, if desired.

CROWNING
TOUCHES

Rich Sauce, Sweet Fruit, Toasted Slivered Almonds

Toppings

ADDED ATTRACTIONS can be found in toppings, glazes, icings, fillings, and sauces—all attention-getters that increase dessert's appeal. The trio of irresistible dessert items pictured on p. 263 are created from (lower left) fresh pineapple chunks, strawberry ice cream, strawberry sauce, and a crunchy contrast of toasted, slivered almonds; (lower right) cantaloupe ring, vanilla ice cream, and blueberry sauce; (top) peach halves, maple-nut ice cream, and caramel butter sauce. The following recipes include many fine ideas for adding variety and appeal to all kinds of desserts.

LEMON-SOUR CREAM TOPPING

Yield: 3-3/4 cups (for 3 9-inch pies)

Ingredients	
LEMON MEDLEY SAUCE	
(See following recipe)	3/4 cup
SOUR CREAM	3 cups
LEMON PEEL, grated	1 tablespoon

Procedure

1. Using wire whip, fold Lemon Medley Sauce into sour cream.
2. Spread on top of baked cooled custard or pumpkin pie allowing about 1-1/4 cups per pie.
3. Sprinkle 1 teaspoon grated lemon peel over each pie.

LEMON MEDLEY SAUCE

Yield: 2 quarts

Ingredients

LEMON PEEL, grated	3 tablespoons
LEMON JUICE, FRESH	1-1/2 cups
SUGAR	1-1/2 quarts
BUTTER	1 pound, 2 ounces
EGGS, slightly beaten	1-1/2 cups

Procedure

1. Combine lemon peel, lemon juice, sugar, and butter. Cook, stirring, over low heat until butter is melted and sugar dissolved.

2. Remove from heat; stir vigorously. Blend 2 cups of mixture into eggs; return all to sauce pan. Cook over low heat, stirring constantly, until mixture is thick. Do not boil.

COCONUT-PECAN TOPPING

Yield: 2 quarts

Ingredients

EVAPORATED MILK	2-1/2 cups
SUGAR, GRANULATED	1-1/4 cups
SUGAR, BROWN (firmly packed)	1-1/4 cups
EGG YOLKS, beaten	2/3 cup
BUTTER *OR* MARGARINE	5/8 cup (5 ounces)
VANILLA	2-1/2 teaspoons
COCONUT, FLAKED	3-1/2 cups
PECANS, chopped	3-1/2 cups

Procedure

1. Combine milk, sugars, and beaten egg yolks in top of double boiler.

2. Cook over hot water until thickened, stirring occasionally (about 20 minutes). Remove from heat.

3. Add butter and vanilla; blend into sauce. Add coconut and pecans; mix well.

4. Use (while warm) to spread over top of cheesecake or custard pies. Cool until served.

ALMOND CRUNCH

Yield: Approximately 3 cups

Ingredients

BUTTER	1 ounce (2 tablespoons)
ALMONDS, blanched, slivered	11 ounces (2-1/2 cups)
SUGAR	9 ounces (1-1/4 cups)

Procedure

1. Melt butter in a large skillet. Stir in almonds. Cook over medium-low heat, stirring constantly, until almonds are light gold in color, about 4 minutes.

2. Stir in sugar; continue to cook, stirring constantly, until sugar coats almonds with a granular crust, melts slightly, and turns golden.

3. Turn out on a marble slab or a sheet of heavy foil. Cool. Break into small pieces.

4. Use as a topping for fruit compotes, ice cream, or frosted cakes; in parfaits, or as a garnish for plain cheesecake.

CEREAL CRUNCH TOPPING

Yield: 3-1/4 pounds mixture

Ingredients

BUTTER	12 ounces
SUGAR, BROWN	1-1/2 pounds
FLOUR	2 ounces
WHOLE WHEAT FLAKES	1 pound (3-3/4 quarts)

Procedure

1. Melt butter in a heavy saucepan. Combine brown sugar and flour; add to butter. Cook, stirring, over low heat 2 minutes, or until sugar melts but does not bubble.

2. Add flakes; mix quickly and thoroughly to coat all flakes. Spread thin in shallow pan. Cool and crumble.

3. Sprinkle over ice cream or use as topping on fudge or fruit sundaes. Or, crumble coarsely and sprinkle over apple sauce, sliced fresh peaches, or bananas. Or, crumble finely and sprinkle over quick coffee cakes or muffins, pressing topping well into batter.

Crunchy Crust and Topping Increase Pie's Appeal

CINNAMON NUT CRUMB TOPPING

Yield: 1-3/4 quarts

Ingredients

BREAD CRUMBS, fine soft	1-1/2 quarts (9-1/2 ounces)
NUTS, finely chopped	1/2 cup
SUGAR	1/3 cup
CINNAMON	2 teaspoons
BUTTER *OR* MARGARINE, melted	1/2 cup

Procedure

1. Combine crumbs, nuts, sugar, and cinnamon.
2. Add melted butter; mix well.
3. Place in a shallow baking pan; bake in oven at 400°F. about 10 minutes, or until toasted.
4. Use to top vanilla or butterscotch puddings, vanilla tapioca cream pudding, or apple sauce.

CINNAMON-CHOCOLATE SOUR CREAM TOPPING

Yield: 1 quart

Ingredients

SEMI-SWEET CHOCOLATE BITS	1-1/2 pounds
SOUR CREAM	1 cup
SALT	1/2 teaspoon
CINNAMON, GROUND	1/2 teaspoon
SUGAR	1/4 cup
VANILLA	1 tablespoon

Procedure

1. Melt chocolate over hot water.
2. Stir in remaining ingredients; blend well. Cool. Serve over plain cake or chocolate ice cream.

PEANUT BRITTLE SOUR CREAM TOPPING

Yield: 2 quarts

Ingredients

CREAM CHEESE	12 ounces
SOUR CREAM	5 cups
ORANGE PEEL, grated	2 tablespoons
PEANUT BRITTLE, crushed	2 cups (9 ounces)

Procedure

1. Whip cream cheese; blend into sour cream.
2. Add orange peel and peanut brittle.
3. Serve a mound of topping (No. 24 scoop) on wedges of pumpkin pie.

SLIVERED FRESH LEMON TOPPING

Yield: 2 quarts

Ingredients

CORNSTARCH	1/2 cup
SUGAR, GRANULATED	1 quart
BUTTER *OR* MARGARINE	1/4 pound
LEMON JUICE	2 cups
WATER, hot	1 quart
LEMON PEEL, grated	2-1/2 tablespoons
LEMONS, sliced into thin slivers	4

Procedure

1. Combine cornstarch and sugar in a 1-gallon saucepan.
2. Add butter, lemon juice, and water. Bring to a boil; cook 3 minutes, stirring to avoid lumping.
3. Add lemon peel and slivered lemon; remove from heat.
4. Serve hot over apple, cherry, peach, or berry pies.

SHERRY-NUTMEG CREAM TOPPING

Yield: 1-1/2 quarts

Ingredients

CREAM, HEAVY	2-1/2 cups
NUTMEG	1-1/2 teaspoons
SHERRY	1/3 cup
CONFECTIONERS' SUGAR	1/4 cup
VANILLA	1 teaspoon

Procedure

1. Combine cream, nutmeg, and sherry; let stand in refrigerator about 30 minutes before whipping.

2. Add sugar and vanilla to unwhipped cream mixture; whip until thick. Chill.

3. Serve a No. 30 scoop of topping on top of slices of pound cake or wedges of apple or blueberry pie.

LINGERING HEAVEN

Yield: 24 portions

Ingredients

DARK SWEET CHERRIES, CANNED	2 quarts
PINEAPPLE CHUNKS, FROZEN (unthawed)	1-1/2 quarts (3-1/4 pounds)
PORT WINE	2 cups
CREAM, HEAVY	1 quart
SUGAR	1/2 cup
RUM FLAVORING	2 teaspoons
CURRANT JELLY, diced	1 cup
ANGEL FOOD CAKE	24 slices

Procedure

1. Drain cherries thoroughly. Combine with unthawed, frozen pineapple and wine. Cover; refrigerate several hours or overnight. Drain.

2. Whip cream with sugar and rum flavoring. Carefully fold in diced jelly and drained fruit.

3. Spoon topping over slices of angel food cake.

ANGEL RASPBERRY FROZEN CREAM

Yield: 20 portions

Ingredients

CREAM, HEAVY	3 cups
SUGAR	3/4 cup
RASPBERRIES, FRESH *OR*	
FROZEN, thawed, drained	3/4 cup
ANGEL FOOD CAKE, 1-inch slices	20

Procedure

1. Beat cream until thickened; add sugar and raspberries. Continue beating until stiff.

2. Drop in mounds on waxed paper or aluminum foil; freeze until firm.

3. Serve slices of angel food topped with raspberry frozen cream.

Note:

If desired, raspberry cream may be served unfrozen.

United Dairy Industry Association

Crunchy Topping Contrasts with Lemon-Pistachio Surprise

ALMOND CREAM TOPPING

Yield: 1-3/4 quarts

Ingredients

CREAM CHEESE, softened	12 ounces
SUGAR, LIGHT BROWN	1/2 pound
SOUR CREAM	1 quart
ALMONDS, sliced, toasted	2 cups
ALMOND EXTRACT	1 teaspoon
ORANGE PEEL, grated	4 teaspoons

Procedure

1. Combine cream cheese and sugar; beat until smooth. Gradually add sour cream.

2. Fold in almonds, almond extract, and orange peel. Chill.

3. Serve over steamed puddings, fruit cake, or lightly sweetened fruit.

SPECIAL SPICED APPLE TOPPING

Yield: 3-3/4 quarts

Ingredients

APPLE SLICES	1 No. 10 can
SUGAR, BROWN	1 pound, 5 ounces
SALT	1 teaspoon
NUTMEG	1-1/2 teaspoons
ALLSPICE	1-1/2 teaspoons
LEMON JUICE	1/2 cup
RAISINS	1-1/2 cups

Procedure

1. Combine ingredients; bring to a boil.

2. Cover; simmer 15 minutes; cool.

3. Serve over sponge or pound cake; top with whipped cream or whipped topping.

FRUIT TOPPING

Yield: 1-1/2 quarts

Ingredients

EGG WHITE	1
FRUIT JUICE, CRUSHED FRUIT,	
OR FRUIT PUREE	1 cup
SUGAR	1 cup

Procedure

1. Beat egg whites, fruit juice (or crushed fruit or fruit puree), and sugar at high speed until ingredients blend, become frothy and thick.

2. Serve as topping over slices of angel food or sponge cake.

Note

Topping stands up for several hours. If it breaks down, rewhip until blended again.

RED RASPBERRY FRUIT WHIP

Yield: Topping for 10 9-inch pies

Ingredients

EGG WHITES	7 ounces
SUGAR	1-3/4 quarts
LEMON JUICE	2-1/3 tablespoons
SALT	2 teaspoons
RED RASPBERRIES, FROZEN,	
thawed	1-3/4 quarts

Procedure

1. Put all ingredients in mixer bowl; beat until fluffy and light and firm peaks form. (Mixture tends to splatter during beating. Use collar on beater, or hold cloth loosely around the bowl.)

2. Use to top vanilla cream pie or pudding, or to top slices of angel food or similar cake.

NO-COOK PLUM TOPPING

Yield: 1-1/2 quarts

Ingredients

CANNED PURPLE PLUMS, drained, pitted, and cut in medium-sized pieces	1 quart
CURRANT JELLY	1-1/2 cups
WALNUTS, chopped	1/2 cup

Procedure

1. Prepare fruit. Whip jelly with a wire whip. Fold in plums and walnuts.

2. Serve as a filling between split squares of plain cake. Garnish with additional plum half and whipped cream or topping, if desired. Or, serve as a sauce over ice cream, individual baked custard, or vanilla pudding.

QUICK FLUFFY TOPPING

Yield: 5 quarts

Ingredients

WHIPPED TOPPING MIX	1 package
INSTANT PUDDING AND PIE FILLING, ANY FLAVOR	1 pound (2-1/2 cups)
MILK, cold	2 quarts
VANILLA	1 tablespoon

Procedure

1. Combine all ingredients in mixer bowl. Blend at low speed for about 30 seconds. Scrape bowl.

2. Whip at high speed until topping will form soft peaks, about 8 minutes.

3. Frost cakes; store in refrigerator.

BROILED PINEAPPLE CAKE TOPPING

Yield: Topping for 2 18-inch by 12-inch cakes

Ingredients

BUTTER *OR* MARGARINE	3/4 pound
PINEAPPLE TIDBITS, drained	1 No. 10 can
COCONUT, SHREDDED	1 cup
SUGAR, BROWN	2 pounds
WALNUTS, chopped	1 pound (1 quart)
BAKED CAKES, 18-inches by	
12-inches by 2-inches	2

Procedure

1. Melt butter; add drained pineapple, coconut, brown sugar, and walnuts. Blend well; spread on cakes.

2. Place under broiler approximately 10 inches from heating unit. Broil slowly until bubbly and lightly browned. Serve warm.

Flavored Whipped Cream and Whipped Toppings

HONEY WHIPPED CREAM

Yield: 1-1/2 quarts

Ingredients

CREAM, HEAVY	3 cups
HONEY	1/3 cup
ALMONDS, slivered, salted, toasted	1 cup

Procedure

1. Whip cream until stiff; blend in honey.
2. Spread on baked, cooled pumpkin or custard pie allowing 9 ounces (about 2 cups) per pie.
3. Sprinkle with almonds.

AMBER WHIPPED CREAM

Yield: 2 quarts

Ingredients

CREAM, HEAVY	1 quart
SUGAR, BROWN, sifted	1 pound
VANILLA	2 teaspoons

Procedure

1. Combine ingredients. Chill 1 hour.
2. Beat until cream holds its shape. Do not overbeat. Spread on top and sides of angel food cake; or use to top plain cake layers or puddings.

COCOA WHIPPED CREAM

Yield: 1 quart

Ingredients

COCOA	1/3 cup
SUGAR	1/3 cup
SALT	1/4 teaspoon
CREAM, HEAVY	2 cups

Procedure

1. Mix cocoa, sugar, and salt. Add cream gradually, stirring to keep mixture smooth. Chill 1 hour.

2. Whip until stiff. Use as a topping for sponge cake or angel food cake, vanilla or chocolate pudding, vanilla or banana cream pie.

RASPBERRY WHIPPED CREAM

Yield: 2 quarts

Ingredients

RASPBERRIES, FRESH*	1-1/2 cups
SUGAR, CONFECTIONERS'	1/4 cup
CREAM, HEAVY	1 quart

Procedure

1. Combine ingredients. Beat until thick. Use as a topping for slices of angel food or pound cake; to garnish portions of vanilla pudding; or as "islands" for floating island.

Use frozen berries, thawed and drained, if desired. Omit sugar.

AMBER TOPPING

Yield: 4-1/2 quarts

Ingredients

SUGAR, BROWN	9 ounces (1-1/4 cups, firmly packed)
VANILLA	1 tablespoon
WHIPPED TOPPING MIX	1 bag

Procedure

1. Add brown sugar and vanilla to topping mix and whip according to directions on bag.

STRAWBERRY WHIPPED CREAM

Yield: Approximately 5 cups

Ingredients

STRAWBERRIES, FROZEN, sliced	1 pound
CREAM, HEAVY	2 cups
SUGAR, CONFECTIONERS'	1/4 cup

Procedure

1. Thaw, drain, and mash berries.
2. Combine cream and confectioners' sugar. Whip only until stiff enough to hold its shape.
3. Carefully fold in drained, mashed berries. Use with angel food cake; white, yellow, or sponge cake layers; simple puddings. Or, use to fill cream puff shells.

United Dairy Industry Association

Cocoa Whipped Cream (Recipe p. 277) Layered with Crisp Meringue. (Recipe p. 141).

COFFEE TOPPING

Yield: 1 quart

Ingredients

SUGAR	2 tablespoons
INSTANT COFFEE	4 teaspoons
WHIPPED TOPPING, prepared	1 quart

Procedure

1. Add sugar and instant coffee to the prepared whipped topping; blend thoroughly.

STRAWBERRY TOPPING

Yield: Approximately 4-1/2 cups

Ingredients

STRAWBERRIES, FROZEN, thawed (with syrup)	2/3 cup
WHIPPED TOPPING, prepared	1 quart
RED FOOD COLORING (optional)	few drops

Procedure

1. Fold the strawberries with their syrup into the whipped topping. Add coloring, if desired, to tint to a delicate shade.

Glazes

BERRY GLAZE

Yield: 3-1/3 cups

Ingredients

SUGAR	6 tablespoons
CORNSTARCH	3 tablespoons
FROZEN BERRIES, thawed, undrained*	1 pound, 14 ounces
LEMON JUICE	1 tablespoon

Procedure

1. Combine sugar and cornstarch. Gradually add berries and lemon juice.

2. Cook, stirring, over medium heat, until thickened. Continue to cook 2 minutes. Cool.

3. Spread over baked, cooled custard pies, allowing 10 ounces per pie.

Strawberries, raspberries, blackberries, or blueberries.

CHOCOLATE GLAZE

Yield: 3/4 cup

Ingredients

BUTTER	2 tablespoons
CHOCOLATE, UNSWEETENED	2 ounces
MILK, hot	3 tablespoons
SUGAR, CONFECTIONERS'	1 cup
SALT	dash

Procedure

1. Melt butter and chocolate slowly over hot water.

2. Combine milk, sugar, and salt; add chocolate mixture gradually, stirring to blend.

3. While glaze is slightly warm, drizzle from tip of iced tea spoon over top of chilled chiffon pie to create a lacy pattern of glaze.

COFFEE GLAZE

Yield: For three 10-inch tube cakes

Ingredients

WATER	1/2 cup
BUTTER	3 tablespoons
SUGAR, CONFECTIONERS', sifted	1 quart
SALT	1/4 teaspoon
INSTANT COFFEE	2 tablespoons

Procedure
1. Heat water and butter together.
2. Mix sugar, salt, and coffee. Add hot liquid; beat until smooth.
3. Spoon over top of cakes, letting glaze run down sides.

CHERRY GLAZE

Yield: For approximately 20 9-inch pies

Ingredients

FROZEN RED CHERRIES	10 pounds
CHERRY JUICE OR WATER	5 quarts
SUGAR	4 pounds, 6 ounces
CLEAR-JEL *OR* TAPIOCA STARCH	1 quart (1 pound, 3 ounces)
SALT	1 tablespoon

Procedure
1. Thaw and drain cherries. Heat juice to boiling.
2. Combine sugar, starch, and salt; add to boiling juice gradually, stirring constantly. Cook until thick, about 15 minutes. Pour over drained cherries.
3. Pour cherry glaze at once over cheesecake or cream pies that have been filled 3/4 full.

SOUR CREAM-NUT GLAZE

Yield: 1-1/2 quarts

Ingredients

SUGAR, LIGHT BROWN	6 ounces
NUTS, toasted, salted, chopped	3/4 cup
SOUR CREAM	4-1/2 cups

Procedure

1. Using a wire whip, fold sugar and nuts into sour cream.

2. Spread on baked, cooled custard or pumpkin pies, allowing about 2 cups per pie.

3. Place pies under broiler. Broil 3 minutes or until cream is glazed and sugar bubbles slightly.

Icings

CHOCOLATE ICING

Yield: 2-1/2 pounds

Ingredients

CONFECTIONER'S SUGAR	2 pounds
CHOCOLATE, UNSWEETENED, melted	1/4 pound
WATER	3/4 cup
SALT	1 teaspoon
VANILLA	1 tablespoon

Procedure

1. Combine sugar, melted chocolate, water, and salt; mix thoroughly. Add vanilla.

2. Spread on eclairs or tops of Boston cream pies.

FLUFFY LIME FROSTING

Yield: Approximately 6-3/4 pounds

Ingredients

BUTTER	1 pound
SALT	1 teaspoon
VANILLA	1-1/2 tablespoons
EGG WHITES, unbeaten	5 (5 ounces)
CONFECTIONER'S SUGAR	5 pounds
LIME JUICE	3/4 cup
LIME PEEL, grated	1/4 cup

Procedure

1. Cream butter, salt, and vanilla; add egg whites.

2. Add confectioner's sugar alternately with lime juice continuing to beat on mixer. Add grated lime peel; beat until of right consistency to spread.

Icings to Please Pint-Size Patrons

Fillings

LEMON CURD

Yield: 3 quarts

Ingredients

BUTTER *OR* MARGARINE	1 pound
LEMON PEEL, grated, from	4 lemons
LEMON JUICE	2 cups
SALT	1 teaspoon
SUGAR	1-1/2 quarts
EGGS, WHOLE	12 (2-1/2 cups)
EGG YOLKS	12 (1 cup)

Procedure

1. Melt butter, add lemon peel and juice, salt, and sugar.
2. Beat whole eggs and yolks together; combine with lemon mixture.
3. Cook over boiling water, stirring constantly, until thick and smooth.

Note

This filling will keep, covered, in the refrigerator for several weeks.

LEMON WHIPPED CREAM FILLING

Yield: 2-1/4 quarts

Ingredients

SUGAR	3 cups
FLOUR, CAKE	1 cup
SALT	1/4 teaspoon
EGG YOLKS	6 (1/2 cup)
WATER	2 cups
LEMON JUICE	1 cup
LEMON PEEL, grated	1 tablespoon
BUTTER	2 tablespoons
CREAM, HEAVY	3 cups

Procedure

1. Combine sugar, flour, and salt in top of double boiler; mix well.

2. Combine egg yolks and water; stir into dry ingredients. Add lemon juice; mix thoroughly.

3. Place over boiling water; cook, stirring, until thickened.

4. Remove from boiling water. Add lemon peel and butter; blend. Cool.

5. Whip cream. Fold into cooled lemon mixture. Use as filling in angel food cakes that have been sliced horizontally into layers. Or, use as topping.

Sauces

CREME FRAICHE

Yield: As desired

Ingredients

BUTTERMILK	1/4 cup
HEAVY CREAM	1 quart; more as needed

Procedure

1. Add buttermilk to 1 quart heavy cream; mix well.
2. Cover and let stand at room temperature 24 hours.
3. Refrigerate another 24 hours before using.
4. For service, stir the mixture, then combine 1 part mixture to 3 parts fresh heavy cream to achieve the amount desired. Serve over fresh fruit.

CREAMY CINNAMON SAUCE

Yield: Approximately 1-1/2 quarts

Ingredients

SUGAR, GRANULATED	1 quart
CINNAMON, GROUND	1 tablespoon
CORN SYRUP, LIGHT	2 cups
WATER	1 cup
EVAPORATED MILK	1-2/3 cups (1 tall can)

Procedure

1. Mix sugar and cinnamon in a large saucepan. Add corn syrup and water.
2. Bring to a full rolling boil over medium heat, stirring constantly. Boil, stirring constantly, 5 minutes or until syrup reaches a temperature of 234°F. Remove from heat.
3. Let cool 5 minutes or until temperature is down to 180°F.
4. Gradually add evaporated milk, blending in with wire whip. Serve warm or cold. (If thinner sauce is desired, add a small amount of hot water.)

FRESH STRAWBERRY AND RHUBARB SAUCE

Yield: 24 portions

Ingredients

RHUBARB, FRESH, diced	3 quarts
WATER	1/2 cup
SALT	1/4 teaspoon
SUGAR	1 quart
LEMON JUICE	1/4 cup
STRAWBERRIES, FRESH, sliced	1-1/2 quarts

Procedure

1. Combine rhubarb, water, and salt. Cover; cook over low heat until rhubarb is tender.

2. Remove from heat; add sugar. Cool.

3. Add lemon juice and strawberries. Serve as a breakfast fruit or as a dessert. Spoon over sliced bananas to vary a familiar theme.

ORANGE-SOUR CREAM SAUCE
(for canned peaches or pineapple)

Yield: 1-1/2 quarts

Ingredients

SOUR CREAM	1 quart
ORANGE PEEL, grated	1/4 cup
ORANGE JUICE	1/2 cup
SUGAR	2 tablespoons
SALT	1/4 teaspoon
SUGAR, BROWN	as needed
MINT SPRIGS, FRESH	as needed

Procedure

1. Combine sour cream, orange peel, orange juice, sugar, and salt. Chill to blend flavors.

2. Serve over drained, chilled fruit. Sprinkle lightly with brown sugar; garnish with mint.

EGGNOG SAUCE

Yield: 1 quart

Ingredients

CREAM, LIGHT	2 cups
EGG YOLKS	4
WHOLE EGGS	2
SALT	1/8 teaspoon
SUGAR	1/3 cup
RUM	1/3 cup
CREAM, HEAVY	1 cup

Procedure

1. Scald light cream over hot water.

2. Beat egg yolks and eggs lightly with salt and sugar. Stir a small amount of the hot cream into the mixture. Combine with remaining cream; cook, stirring constantly, until mixture thickens and coats spoon.

3. Remove from heat; cool thoroughly. Add rum. Chill.

4. Whip cream until thick and shiny but not stiff. Fold into custard mixture.

National Cherry Growers and Industries Association

Dramatic Sauce of Dark, Sweet Cherries

MINCEMEAT SAUCE

Yield: Approximately 2 quarts

Ingredients

SUGAR	2 cups
WATER	2 cups
MARASCHINO CHERRIES, chopped	1 cup
MINCEMEAT, prepared	1 quart
WALNUTS, chopped	1 cup

Procedure

1. Dissolve sugar in water; boil 5 minutes.
2. Remove from heat; add cherries, mincemeat, and nuts. Serve warm over baked apples or ice cream.

CHERRY SAUCE

Yield: 50 1-oz. portions

Ingredients

RED PITTED CHERRIES, FROZEN (SYRUP PACK)	3-1/2 pounds
CHERRY JUICE AND WATER, to equal	3-3/4 cups
SUGAR	1 cup
CORNSTARCH	1/4 cup
SALT	1/2 teaspoon
LEMON JUICE	2 tablespoons
ALMOND EXTRACT	1 teaspoon
RED FOOD COLORING	as desired

Procedure

1. Defrost cherries. Drain; measure liquid. Add water to make 3-3/4 cups.
2. Mix sugar, cornstarch, and salt. Add to cherry juice and water. Cook, stirring until mixture comes to a boil. Boil 1/2 minute.
3. Remove from heat. Add drained cherries, lemon juice, almond extract, and red food coloring.
4. Cool; serve over custard, squares of plain cake (for cottage pudding), bread pudding, ice cream, or cherry pie a la mode.

SPARKLING STRAWBERRY SAUCE

Yield: 1-1/4 gallons

Ingredients

GELATIN, STRAWBERRY FLAVOR	12 ounces (1-3/4 cups)
WATER, hot	2 quarts
STRAWBERRIES, FROZEN, sliced, juice included	6-1/2 pounds (3 quarts)

Procedure

1. Dissolve gelatin in hot water. Add berries.
2. Chill until ready to serve. Serve on ice cream, cake, or pudding.

Note

If sauce becomes too thick, let stand at room temperature a few minutes before serving.

LEMON SAUCE I

Yield: 1-1/2 quarts

Ingredients

LEMON PUDDING OR PIE FILLING, cooked (hot)	1 quart
WATER, hot	2 cups
LEMON, thin slices, quartered	2 lemons

Procedure

1. Add water to hot pudding; blend. Add quartered slices of lemon.
2. Serve warm over apple pie, or over slices of pound, angel food, chiffon, or sponge cake.

LEMON SAUCE II

Yield: 1-1/2 quarts

Ingredients

SUGAR	2 cups
SALT	1/2 teaspoon
CORNSTARCH	2/3 cup
WATER, boiling	1 quart
LEMON PEEL, grated	1-1/2 tablespoons
LEMON JUICE	1/4 cup
BUTTER *OR* MARGARINE	1/4 pound

Procedure

1. Mix sugar, salt, and cornstarch; add to boiling water.
2. Cook, stirring, over low heat until thickened and clear.
3. Remove from heat. Add lemon peel, lemon juice, and butter. Use over warm Dutch apple pie, apple cobbler, or gingerbread.

CHERRY MAPLE SAUCE

Yield: Approximately 1 quart

Ingredients

CHERRY PIE FILLING	1 quart
MAPLE EXTRACT	1 tablespoon

Procedure

1. Blend ingredients thoroughly but carefully, avoiding breaking up fruit.
2. If desired, thin slightly with warm water.

WINE FRUIT SAUCE FOR FLOATING ISLAND

Yield: 50 portions

Ingredients

RED GRAPES	2 pounds
TANGERINES	8
PEARS	8
APPLES	8
ORANGES	8
BANANAS	6
FRESH STRAWBERRIES	1-1/2 quarts
LEMON JUICE	1/4 cup
SUGAR	1 pound
WATER	2 cups
WHOLE CLOVES	8
WHOLE CINNAMON	1 4-inch stick
NUTMEG	1/2 teaspoon
CURRANT JELLY	1 cup
FRESH ORANGE JUICE	2 cups
ORANGE PEEL	2 tablespoons
FRESH LEMON JUICE	1/4 cup
CORNSTARCH *OR* ARROWROOT	2 tablespoons
CLARET *OR* BURGUNDY	2 cups
KIRSCH (optional)	1-1/2 cups

Procedure

1. Wash and cut grapes in half; seed. Section tangerines. Peel pears, apples, oranges, and bananas; cut in large dice. Cut strawberries in halves or, if large, in quarters. Add first amount of lemon juice to fruit.

2. Combine sugar, water, spices, jelly, and orange juice and peel in saucepan; bring to boil, stirring frequently. Blend second amount of lemon juice with cornstarch; stir into boiling liquid. Cook 5 minutes.

3. Cool; add wine and Kirsch. Add fruit.

4. When serving, place 1/2 cup of vanilla pudding in a sherbet or dessert dish. Place a mound of baked soft meringue in the center and the wine fruit sauce around it.

LEMON SAUCE
(for Swedish Cream, recipe p. 246)

Yield: Approximately 1 quart

Ingredients

LEMON PIE FILLING	1 quart
WATER, warm	1 cup
NUTMEG	as needed

Procedure

1. Blend water, a little at a time, into pie filling.
2. Serve at room temperature over unmolded Swedish Cream. Sprinkle portions lightly with nutmeg.

PEACH ALMOND SAUCE

Yield: Approximately 1 quart

Ingredients

PEACH PIE FILLING	1 quart
ALMOND EXTRACT	2 to 3 teaspoons
WATER, warm (optional)	as needed
ALMONDS, slivered (optional)	as needed

Procedure

1. Blend pie filling and extract thoroughly but carefully, avoiding breaking up fruit.
2. If desired, thin slightly with warm water.
3. Serve over Swedish Cream (recipe p. 246) or other desserts.
4. If desired, garnish portions with slivered almonds.

PINEAPPLE MINT SAUCE

Yield: Approximately 1 quart

Ingredients

PINEAPPLE PIE FILLING	1 quart
CREME DE MENTHE, GREEN	1/4 cup

Procedure

Blend ingredients thoroughly but carefully, avoiding breaking up fruit.

DESSERT CHEESES

Cheese for Dessert

CHEESE FOR DESSERT adds a note of elegance to the menu. What's more, it offers an opportunity for showmanship when presented with finesse.

The menu listing can be as simple as one kind of cheese teamed with a few crackers and a companionable fruit, such as a piece of well-ripened Camembert with toasted crackers and wedges of red-skinned apple. Or the service can be made more elaborate—and impressive—by offering a choice of cheeses and fruit attractively arranged on a tray carried to the table or wheeled up on a cart. Either way, cheese easily qualifies as a "quick-to-fix" dessert: there's no cooking involved, and preparation time is practically nil.

Cheese-loving patrons enjoy a selection of cheeses presented with seasonable fresh fruit, delicate-flavored crackers, and perhaps some slices of crisp-crusted bread. Connoisseurs will also appreciate a cup of robust black coffee or a glass of appropriate wine.

There's plenty of leeway in planning a cheese board or tray. Attention can be focused on a few well-chosen cheeses or on a variety of kinds. The cheese can be presented in portions or left in large pieces to be sliced at the table to conform with the diners' appetite. When choosing the selection, keep in mind variety and contrast in flavor, color, texture, and shape. To serve the cheese at its best, always allow it to stand at room temperature to soften texture, enhance flavor, and release aroma. Small wedges of foil-wrapped soft cheese may need only 20 minutes or so, but larger pieces may take as much as an hour.

Arrange the cheeses to show off to advantage with some eye-catching contrast. A few green leaves, tucked in here and there, add color and help emphasize the various pieces of cheese.

The fruits to co-star with cheese should always be excellent examples of their kind. They should be ripened to the right stage for maximum eating pleasure.

The accompanying chart suggests a number of delightful cheese and fruit combinations, but it by no means is claimed to be complete. There are other cheeses, other fruits, to extend the list. Additional combinations merit trying: good cheese, well-presented, is always a worthy finish to a meal.

Washington Growers Association

Fruit and Cheese, a Favorite Finale

DOMESTIC AND IMPORTED DESSERT CHEESE

Type	Origin	Description	Accompaniment
Cream	U.S.A.	Surface: white, no crust. Interior: white, smooth texture, soft. Flavor: delicate, slightly acid. 3-6-8 oz. packages. Loaf	Crackers of delicate flavor, pears, apples, grapes, dates, figs, prunes, jelly or preserves, pre-served kumquats, fresh straw-berries, peaches
Liederkranz *Trade-mark name*	U.S.A.	Surface: russet. Interior: creamy yellow, soft. Flavor and aroma: robust. Rectangular foil wrapped package 4 oz.	Crackers of all types, tokay grapes
Monterey Jack	U.S.A.	Surface: grayish white. Interior: white, semi-soft. Flavor: mild. Circular wheels 10 lbs. Rindless block 10 to 40 lbs.	Crackers of all types, apples, pears, grapes
Oka *or* Port du Salut	Canada	Surface: russet. Interior: creamy yellow, semi-soft Circular cake 1 lb., 5 lbs.	Crackers of delicate flavor, pears, apples, grapes

Name	Origin	Description	Serve with
Aged Cheddar	England	Surface: waxed yellow brown. Interior: light yellow to orange, semi-hard. Flavor: pronounced. Circular, cylindrical, or block form 5 to 70 lbs.	Crackers of all types, apples, pears
Roquefort (*Roke-fort*)	France	Surface: yellowish-brown. Interior: white with blue-green mold, semi-soft. Flavor: salty and piquant. Cylindrical, foil wrapped 4-1/2 to 6 lbs.	Crackers of all types, pears, apples, grapes, peaches, nuts
Blue (spelled *Bleu* on imported cheese)	France	Surface: foil wrapped. Interior: veined with green mold, semi-soft. Flavor: piquant Cylindrical 5 lbs.	Crackers of all types, apples, fresh pears, salted nuts
Brie (*Bree*)	France	Surface: russet brown. Interior: creamy yellow, soft. (surface ripened) Circular cake 2-4-6 lbs.	Crackers of delicate flavor, pears, tokay grapes, apples, peaches
Camembert (*Kam-em-bear*)	France	Surface: thin, whitish crust. Interior: creamy yellow, soft. Flavor: mellow, but robust. Circular cake. Individual portions.	Crackers of delicate flavor, pears, apples, tart plums, pineapple

Type	Origin	Description	Accompaniment
Bel Paese (*Bell-pa-azey'*)	Italy	Surface: slate grey. Interior: light yellow, soft. Flavor: mild. Flat circular cake. 1 lb. and 5 lbs.	Crackers of delicate flavor, apples, grapes, pears
Gorgonzola	Italy	Surface: light tan. Interior: light yellow with green mold, semi-hard. Flavor: rich piquant. Cylindrical 16 to 19 lbs.	Crackers of all types, pears, apples, grapes
Edam (*Ee-dam*)	North Holland	Surface: red-coated. Interior: creamy yellow, semi-hard. Flavor: mild. Slightly salty when fresh, pronounced when cured. Cannon ball or loaf 2 to 6 lbs.	Crackers of delicate flavor, pears, apples, oranges, tangerines
Gjetost (*Yea-toast'*)	Norway	Interior: light brown, semi-hard. Flavor: sweetish. Cubical and rectangular. 8 oz. and 1 lb.	Thin slices (shaved off) with crackers
Gouda (*Goó'da*)	South Holland	Surface: red-coated. Interior: creamy yellow, semi-hard. Flavor: similar to Edam Flattened ball 12 to 16 oz., 2 to 5 lbs.	Crackers of delicate flavor, pears, apples, oranges, grapes

| Gruyere (*Grew-yare'*) | Switzerland | Interior: light yellow, semi-hard
Flavor: nut sweet
50 to 100 lb. wheels. 8 oz. package.
Usually processed and sold in foil wrapped individual portions | Crackers of delicate flavor, oranges, tangerines · |
| Mysost | Scandinavia | Interior: light brown, semi-hard.
Flavor: mild, sweetish, distinct aroma
Cubical and cylindrical 8 oz. 1 lb., 18 lbs. | Thin slices (shaved off) with crackers |

Index